PUBLIUS VIRGILIUS MARO

THE GEORGICS

TRANSLATED INTO ENGLISH VERSE
BY JOHN DRYDEN
WITH AN INTRODUCTION BY GEORGE F. WHICHER
AND ILLUSTRATIONS
BY BRUNO BRAMANTI

NEW YORK : THE HERITAGE PRESS

INTRODUCTION

Virgil's lifetime, B. C. 70 to 19, coincided with the death throes of the Roman Republic. He was twenty-six when Julius Cæsar was assassinated, thirty-nine when Octavian triumphed at Actium. He lived to see the victor assume the title of Cæsar Augustus and consolidate the Roman rule over most of the known world. Only once was he personally affected by the tumultuous events of his age, when he was dispossessed of his farm near Mantua in order that veterans might be settled on the land. But powerful friends soon came to his relief. Under the protection of the great Mæcenas he was enabled to live a retired, scholarly life quite apart from the court intrigues that seethed around him. As his epitaph states, he wrote successively of pastoral life, of country things, and of deeds of arms. His final masterpiece, in which he related the legend of the coming of Trojan refugees to Italy, both foretold the glory of imperial Rome and measured the human cost of 'the doubtful doom of man'. He is said to have considered it far from finished at the time of his death. Previously he had perfected and published a different kind of poem, *The Georgics*, which is loosely comparable to such English poems as James Thomson's *The Seasons* and William Cowper's *The Task*.

Didactic poetry, so diligently cultivated by eighteenth century poets between Dryden and Wordsworth, has been out of favor now for well over a century. It is easier, consequently, for modern readers to appreciate Virgil's *Bucolics*, written in the pastoral vein of Theocritus, and the *Aeneid*, which borrows its epic plumes from Homer, than to give sympathetic attention to the poem wherein he celebrates the fourfold labors of the farm. Yet the *Georgics* has not lacked distinguished admirers, among them Montaigne and Dryden, Robert Burns, who probably echoed Dryden's opinion, and Edna St. Vincent Millay, who assuredly did not. What reasons can be offered for the decisive preference expressed by such a varied group of judges?

If we follow the line of contemporary esthetics, one consideration immediately suggests itself. A didactic poem has no preconceived framework, narrative or otherwise, and few formal conventions. If the material to be transmuted into poetry is by nature commonplace and unglamorous, it presents a maximum challenge to the poet. He must shape the poem from beginning to end on his own responsibility. There will not be a moment when he can afford to relax and let the momentum of the poem carry him along. Whatever success he achieves finally will be a triumph of sheer craftsmanship. In this respect didactic poetry may be said to share the advantages which modernist painters see in abstract and non-representational art. The *Georgics* belongs more intimately to Virgil than even the last six books of the *Aeneid*, where he has shaken off Homeric leading strings. Dryden called it not inadvisedly 'the best poem of the best poet'. It remains for us to interpret what he meant by 'best'.

He did not mean, of course, most original, as though the *Georgics* were something new and unparalleled in the world, without precedent or sources. No classical Latin poem was original in that sense. Virgil explicitly declares that he hopes 'to sing through Roman towns the song of Ascra', or in other words to adapt the poems of Hesiod to Latin verse. But if the *Works and Days* of the old Greek poet served him as a model, it was one that he soon abandoned. At most his indebtedness is confined to some portions of his first Book, since the only phase of agriculture that Hesiod discussed in the poems that have come down to us was the cultivation of the fields. Yet undoubtedly Virgil had many other sources from which he borrowed material or suggestions. The invocation to the gods at the beginning of his poem is apparently based on a similar passage in Varro's prose tract, *De Re Rustica*; the signs of good and bad weather are drawn from the *Prognostics* of Aratus; the description at the close of the third Book, of the murrain that decimated the livestock of northern Italy, is consciously parallel to the account of the plague of Athens in Lucretius, which in turn is borrowed from Thucydides. It would be possible, using only what remains of classical poetry have survived to our own day, to extend this list of monuments from which Virgil took stones for his own building. When we reflect that among works available to him but not to us was a lost *Georgics* by the Greek poet Nicander, who also wrote a poem on bee-culture, we are forced to resign any thought of setting up Virgil as the originator of specific factual details. The plain fact is that he borrowed more than scholars can trace.

Such procedure, however illegitimate it would seem today, was normal and expected in classical times, when the writing of poetry was often regarded as a kind of rhetorical exercise. Poets showed their skill by paraphrasing other poets, by turning prose works into verse, and by translating from the Greek. Among these *metaphrastes* or 'rehashing' versifiers was the Aratus mentioned above as one of Virgil's sources. Besides his *Prognostics* he wrote a metrical version of an astronomical treatise by Eudoxus, and Cicero, who translated the work into Latin, remarked that here was a man who knew nothing of astronomy but had made a good poem on the stars. Though both Virgil and Aratus made free with whatever materials they could find, there was a profound difference between them, which Professor Conington has exactly defined by saying that the object of Aratus was to impart information, while that of Virgil was to give pleasure by creating a thing of beauty. The difference can be further illustrated if we put the *Georgics* beside Thomas Tusser's *A Hundred Good Points of Husbandry*, published in 1557, which aims to supply the farmer with easily memorable adages.

Once a true idea of the poet's function is clearly grasped, all attempts to find an economic motive for the writing of the *Georgics* will come to seem not so much unfounded as irrelevant. There is an ingenious theory that the statesmanlike Mæcenas prompted Virgil to write a poem in praise of agriculture in order to stimulate the growing of wheat. Italy was facing a food shortage. Wholesale dispossession of farmers and the giving of their lands as bonuses to returning soldiers had taken many farms out of production. While the grain locally grown was insufficient to supply the population, Sextus Pompeius, a first-class pirate, with a navy based on Sicily, was in a position to cut Rome off from its bread-basket in Africa. The theory accounts for everything except the nature of the poem that Virgil produced. Only a fourth part of his work deals with the raising of grain. If his main intention had been to write a versified manual of agriculture, his procedure was curiously inept, since instead of supplementing and expanding his sources he almost invariably abbreviated what he drew from them. Furthermore he neglected entirely one of the most important aspects of Roman farm management, namely the overseeing of a labor force, a matter that fills many pages in the practical books of Cato and Varro. To listen to Virgil you might suppose that every Roman farmer was a Cincinnatus guiding his own plow.

The *Georgics* resembles nothing so much as a magnificent set of tapestries, of which the subject is the four parts of husbandry. A considerable portion of the detail woven into the designs is realistic, but intermixed with representations of the typical occupations of the plowman, the wine-grower, the herdsman, and the bee-keeper are mythological figures and purely decorative arabesques portraying leaves, flowers, birds, insects, little animals, lizards, and snakes. Some features of the patterns are traditional, yet that fact does not detract from the glory of the work. Its glory is cumulative and culminating. Here lesser works of a similar kind have their fruition, the parts are justly proportioned, the colors harmonized, and every thread in the enormous fabric is rightly placed. By some such analogy as this we may suggest the quality of Virgil's achievement in composing a poem which is said to have occupied him for seven years. He is the best poet in the sense that he absorbs and utilizes with deliberate and conscious artistry the best of what has previously been done. It is the best poem because it supplies the finishing touches that perfect the labor of generations.

Virgil is the very type of self-conscious literary artist, a poet's poet if there ever was one. Homer has no being apart from the *Iliad* and the *Odyssey*; indeed it is possible to sustain the illusion that these poems have come into existence without personal agency, so indistinguishable is the workman from the work, the dancer from the dance. But Virgil is like a concert pianist at the keyboard; part of the pleasure lies in watching the dexterity of his hands.

The art needful for the shaping of a didactic poem is a kind of exalted tact, a sense of proper proportion and timing, of climax and contrast, of tone and modulation. The subject should be developed less by logical progression than by a seemingly casual association of topics. The reader's attention like a shuttlecock in air must be kept up by repeated skillful strokes. Every resource of variety must be brought into play. This is where Virgil is most deft. Like his own warrior maid Camilla he flies over the grain fields so lightly that not a stalk is bent. In contrast Lucretius, with the advantage of a great meaningful subject, often drags himself heavily through a long succession of monotonous lines.

Some perception of Virgil's constructive mastery can be gained by studying the diversified organization evidenced in the four parts of his poem, where he is facing a problem akin to that encountered by T. S. Eliot in the *Four Quartets*. He must play the same tune four times over without letting it degenerate into mechanical repetition.

The opening lines of the first Book announce as briefly as possible the subject of the whole poem. There follows – and this feature is repeated in each section – an invocation appropriate to the particular topic about to be discussed. In the body of Book I the poetic evocation of plowing, sowing, and harvesting the grain is framed as it were between two consciously contrasted panels, a bright picture of the earth awakening in spring and a dark picture of autumn bringing the storm. The work of the fields is lightly sketched. Since the Golden Age of Saturn is no more, toil is the lot of mortals. Let the workman therefore look well to his tools. Of all the multifarious equipment discussed at length in the prose manuals on farming Virgil treats only the making of the plow and the constructing of a threshing-floor. He then chronicles the operations of the plowman's year as timed by the rising and setting of the stars, adding a picture of indoor occupations suitable for seasons of bad weather. A list of lucky and unlucky days and hours introduces the storm scene, and Book I modulates to a close through a series of instructions to the weatherwise and a prayer for peace and prosperity in troubled times.

Book II on the cultivation of trees and vines begins with an invocation to Bacchus. Much of this section is purely factual: the various kinds of trees, how to plant and graft them, the proper soil for each kind and how to test it, the planting of a vineyard and the tending and dressing of the vines, olive culture, fruit trees and other trees useful for browse or timber. But these somewhat pedestrian matters are three times interrupted by digressions evidently calculated to quicken and intensify the poem. The first is an exhortation to husbandmen to be up and doing, even as Virgil himself is toiling at the bidding of Mæcenas. The second, rising naturally from the mention of soil, is a patriotic apostrophe to the land of Italy. The third and longest, which concludes the section, celebrates the advantages of country life and contrasts the farmer's cheerful occupations with the toils and dangers of politics, commerce, and war.

Flocks and herds, under the protection of Pales and Apollo, next concern the poet. Book III is particularly notable as including a succession of brilliant little vignettes or set pieces of description. A cow with all the points of a good breeder, a likely colt, a chariot race, a bull overpowered by his rival and driven from the herd, the deer on the wintry plains of Scythia impounded in the snow, the adder lurking in the refuse of the stable, the sick ox dying in the furrow – these stand out most vividly. A discussion of animal diseases and their remedies leads up to the frightful account of pestilence-stricken cattle and sheep, which forms an effective contrast with the idyllic life of the farmer pictured at the end of the preceding book.

A tactful dedication to Mæcenas, with Apollo favoring, opens the final section, which treats of apiculture. Until fairly recent times the life history of the bee, as Maeterlinck has delightfully described it, was very imperfectly understood. Virgil embodies in his lines all the popular misapprehensions along with much practical advice on the methods of caring for the hives. Early in the book he inserts a brief digression on gardens, which includes his reference to an old Corycian settled near Tarentum, who has transformed a few acres of sub-marginal land into a small paradise of greenery, fruits, and flowers. At the end of this book comes the longest digression of all, an epyllion or miniature epic story telling how the culture-hero Aristæus, king of Arcadia, recovered fresh swarms of bees when his hives were emptied as a punishment for his having caused the death of Eurydice, the well-beloved wife of Orpheus.

By way of epilogue Virgil recalls the reader from the legendary past to the events of his own day, the aftermath of the defeat of Antony and Cleopatra at Actium:

While mighty Caesar, thund'ring from afar,
Seeks on Euphrates' banks the spoils of war . . .
On the glad earth the golden age renews,
And his great father's path to heaven pursues.

There is never a hint of a flaw in Virgil's expressions of loyalty to Cæsar, yet we have reason to wonder if he could have written these lines with unmixed feelings. Originally, according to the commentary of Servius, he had ended the *Georgics* with a eulogistic tribute to his friend Cornelius Gallus, whom he had already celebrated in the sixth and tenth eclogues of his *Bucolics*. Gallus took part in the battle of Actium and remained in Egypt as Roman prefect. Then for reasons unknown he fell into disfavor with Octavian and was so harshly disciplined that he committed suicide. Virgil discreetly withdrew the lines in praise of his dead friend and substituted a harmless Greek legend. Harmless, yet it framed the tale of a singer who braved Hades in hope to recover a loved shade.

The richness of the poem's texture in minor ways can be realized only by a reading of the text. Like Keats in *Endymion* Virgil was evidently determined that in perfecting his work he would 'load every rift with ore'. He associates the restricted labors of the farm with images of cosmic scope: with the rising and setting of the heavenly bodies, with the names of distant places and peoples, with myths of gods and heroes, with the wars of the Titans, and even with human battles long ago and some more recent. His imagination revels in lists: the small living creatures that infest threshing-floors or stables, the kinds of grapes and the wines made from them, names of Italian lakes, famous families, horses noted in story, birds that portend a change of weather, the enemies of bees. When he speaks of the river-nymph Cyrene, mother of Aristæus, he adds at once a galaxy of twelve more nymphs whose names are twelve sweet symphonies. And on occasion he heightens the animation of his work by full-fledged epic similes – the helpless charioteer behind his runaway steeds at the end of Book I, and in Book IV the smithy of the Cyclopes compared with the labors of the hive. All these allusions supply harmonic effects. The *Georgics* is not a simple melody piped on a rustic flute.

What has been said hitherto applies to the poem as it exists in the original Latin or in a competent translation, of which there are many. To connoisseurs of Latin poetry, however, the chief beauties of Virgil (as of any great poet) are untranslatable. They reside in the ineffable felicity of diction, variation of pause and rhythm, patterns of assonance, delicate management of what Robert Frost calls 'images to the ear', and other graces of expression so subtle that they defy analysis. Perhaps a trivial example may serve to convey some notion of the values inevitably lost in translation. When Virgil writes:

> *. . . saepe exiguus mus*
> *sub terris posuitque domos atque horrea fecit,*

he has contrived a threefold effect of humor. There is first the witty implication that the miniscule operations of the mouse below ground are a parody in little of the heavy labors of the farm above. Second, by the verbal incongruity of a pedantic adjective linked to an inconsiderable noun (*exiguus mus*, the imponderable mouse), and, third, by the intentional discord of two like sounds in immediate proximity (*-us mus*; the two syllables form a spondee) he invites us to share his smile. Any doubt that humor is intended is resolved by the fact that Horace imitated the same effect in an even more broadly humorous context:

> *parturiunt montes, nascetur ridiculus mus.*

Under heavy-handed analysis, of course, any inclination to smile is dissipated, but imagine what it would be like to stumble suddenly upon such a combination of wit, incongruity, and tonal absurdity. To an alert mind the effect would be like a burst of fireworks. In Dryden's rendering, however, the fireworks don't go off:

> *The field-mouse builds her garner under ground*
> *For gathered grain . . .*

Yet Dryden's translation, on the whole, is one of the best. He will sometimes conventionalize Virgil's language, as when he writes:

> *And thou, for whom the Cean shore sustains*
> *The milky herds, that graze the flowery plains,*

when the original literally reads: 'Thou for whom three hundred snow-white bullocks crop the lush thickets of Cea.' We can forgive him much, however, for the brilliance of such openings as the lines at the start of Book I:

> *What makes a plenteous harvest, when to turn*
> *The fruitful soil, and when to sow the corn;*
> *The care of sheep, of oxen, and of kine,*
> *And how to raise on elms the teeming vine;*
> *The birth and genius of the frugal bee,*
> *I sing, Maecenas, and I sing to thee.*

This is poetry in its own right.

It remains to call attention to two features of the *Georgics* which offset the possible dryness of didactic verse by introducing a more personal note. Several times Virgil speaks of his own preferences or ambitions, and always with lyrical fervor. Toward the close of Book II he prays that his mind may be enlightened to know the causes of natural phenomena, eclipses, earthquakes, and the like, as though he were hoping to rival Lucretius on his own ground. In the following book his words seem to imply that he is planning a poem in honor of Cæsar's conquests. In any event he intends to abandon the hackneyed themes of Grecian poetry:

> *New ways I must attempt, my grovelling name*
> *To raise aloft, and wing my flight to fame.*
> *I, first of Romans, shall in triumph come*
> *From conquered Greece and bring her trophies home,*
> *With foreign spoils adorn my native place*
> *And with Idume's palms my Mantua grace.*

xv

Of Parian stone a temple I will raise,
Where the slow Mincius through the valley strays,
Where cooling streams invite the flocks to drink,
And reeds defend the winding water's brink.

Virgil's desire for personal renown is fused with a depth of patriotic feeling unique, as far as I am aware, in classical literature. The longing of Odysseus for rocky Ithaca is an exile's wish to return to his own fireside, wife, and familiar station. The emotion that Pericles feels for Athens is an intellectual pride in its achievements and free life of the mind. But Virgil's patriotism is instinctive, a sheer love of the soil itself, an unreasoning passionate attachment to the fatherland which seems to mark the birth of a nationalism akin to nationalistic sentiment as we know it today. In the multifarious harmonies of the *Georgics* this is the dominant chord:

But neither Median woods (a plenteous land),
Fair Ganges, Hermus rolling golden sand,
Nor Bactria, nor the richer Indian fields,
Nor all the gummy stores Arabia yields,
Nor any foreign earth of greater name,
Can with sweet Italy contend in fame . . .
Hail, sweet Saturnian soil! of fruitful grain
Great parent, greater of illustrious men!
For thee my tuneful accents will I raise,
And treat of arts disclosed in ancient days.

Tennyson in his beautiful commemorative tribute to this 'landscape-lover, lord of language' perfectly characterized the poet when he called him 'Roman Virgil'.

GEORGE F. WHICHER

VIRGIL'S GEORGICS

THE FIRST GEORGIC

THE ARGUMENT

The poet, in the beginning of this book, propounds the general design of each Georgic: and, after a solemn invocation of all the gods who are any way related to his subject, he addresses himself, in particular, to Augustus, whom he compliments with divinity; and after strikes into his business. He shews the different kinds of tillage proper to different soils; traces out the original of agriculture; gives a catalogue of the husbandman's tools; specifies the employments peculiar to each season; describes the changes of the weather, with the signs in heaven and earth that forebode them; instances many of the prodigies that happened near the time of Julius Caesar's death; and shuts up all with a supplication to the gods for the safety of Augustus, and the preservation of Rome.

What makes a plenteous harvest, when to turn
The fruitful soil, and when to sow the corn;
The care of sheep, of oxen, and of kine;
And how to raise on elms the teeming vine;
The birth and genius of the frugal bee,
I sing, Mæcenas, and I sing to thee.
  Ye deities! who fields and plains protect,
Who rule the seasons, and the year direct,
Bacchus and fostering Ceres, powers divine,
Who gave us corn for mast, for water, wine:
Ye Fauns, propitious to the rural swains,
Ye Nymphs that haunt the mountains and the plains,
Join in my work, and to my numbers bring
Your needful succor; for your gifts I sing.
And thou, whose trident struck the teeming earth,
And made a passage for the courser's birth;
And thou, for whom the Cean shore sustains

The milky herds that graze the flowery plains;
And thou, the shepherds' tutelary god,
Leave, for awhile, O Pan! thy loved abode;
And, if Arcadian fleeces be thy care,
From fields and mountains to my song repair.
Inventor, Pallas, of the fattening oil,
Thou founder of the plough, and ploughman's toil;
And thou, whose hands the shroud-like cypress rear:
Come, all ye gods and goddesses, that wear
The rural honors, and increase the year;
You, who supply the ground with seeds of grain;
And you, who swell those seeds with kindly rain;
And chiefly thou, whose undetermined state
Is yet the business of the gods' debate,
Whether in after-times to be declared
The patron of the world, and Rome's peculiar guard,
Or o'er the fruits and seasons to preside,
And the round circuit of the year to guide —
Powerful of blessings, which thou strew'st around,
And with thy goddess-mother's myrtle crowned.
Or wilt thou, Cæsar, choose the watery reign,
To smooth the surges, and correct the main?
Then mariners, in storms, to thee shall pray;
E'en utmost Thulè shall thy power obey;
And Neptune shall resign the fasces of the sea.
The watery virgins for thy bed shall strive,
And Tethys all her waves in dowry give,
Or wilt thou bless our summers with thy rays,

And, seated near the Balance, poise the days,
Where, in the void of heaven, a space is free,
Betwixt the Scorpion and the Maid, for thee?
The Scorpion, ready to receive thy laws,
Yields half his region, and contracts his claws.
Whatever part of heaven thou shalt obtain
(For let not hell presume of such a reign;
Nor let so dire a thirst of empire move
Thy mind, to leave thy kindred gods above;
Though Greece admires Elysium's blest retreat,
Though Proserpine affects her silent seat,
And, importuned by Ceres to remove,
Prefers the fields below to those above),
Be thou propitious, Cæsar! guide my course,
And to my bold endeavors add thy force:
Pity the poet's and the ploughman's cares;
Interest thy greatness in our mean affairs,
And use thyself betimes to hear and grant our prayers.
   While yet the spring is young, while earth unbinds
Her frozen bosom to the western winds;
While mountain snows dissolve against the sun,
And streams yet new, from precipices run;
E'en in this early dawning of the year,
Produce the plough, and yoke the sturdy steer,
And goad him till he groans beneath his toil,
Till the bright share is buried in the soil.
That crop rewards the greedy peasant's pains,
Which twice the sun, and twice the cold sustains,

And bursts the crowded barns with more than promised
But, ere we stir the yet unbroken ground,   [gains.
The various course of seasons must be found;
The weather, and the setting of the winds,
The culture suiting to the several kinds
Of seeds and plants, and what will thrive and rise,
And what the genius of the soil denies.
This ground with Bacchus, that with Ceres, suits:
That other loads the trees with happy fruits:
A fourth, with grass unbidden, decks the ground.
Thus Tmolus is with yellow saffron crowned:
India black ebon and white ivory bears;
And soft Idumè weeps her od'rous tears.
Thus Pontus sends her beaver-stones from far;
And naked Spaniards temper steel for war:
Epirus, for the Elean chariot, breeds
(In hopes of palms) a race of running steeds.
   This is the original contract; these the laws
Imposed by Nature, and by Nature's cause,
On sundry places, when Deucalion hurled
His mother's entrails on the desert world;
Whence men, a hard laborious kind, were born.
Then borrow part of winter for thy corn,
And early, with thy team, the glebe in furrows turn;
That, while the turf lies open and unbound,
Succeeding suns may bake the mellow ground.
But, if the soil be barren, only scar
The surface, and but lightly print the share,

When cold Arcturus rises with the sun;
Lest wicked weeds the corn should overrun
In watery soils; or lest the barren sand
Should suck the moisture from the thirsty land.
Both these unhappy soils the swain forbears,
And keeps a sabbath of alternate years,
That the spent earth may gather heart again,
And, bettered by cessation, bear the grain.
At least where vetches, pulse, and tares, have stood,
And stalks of lupines grew (a stubborn wood),
The ensuing season, in return, may bear
The bearded product of the golden year:
For flax and oats will burn the tender field,
And sleepy poppies harmful harvests yield.
But sweet vicissitudes of rest and toil
Make easy labor, and renew the soil.
Yet sprinkle sordid ashes all around,
And load with fattening dung thy fallow ground.
Thus change of seeds for meagre soils is best;
And earth manured, not idle, though at rest.
   Long practice has a sure improvement found,
With kindled fires to burn the barren ground,
When the light stubble, to the flames resigned,
Is driven along, and crackles in the wind.
Whether from hence the hollow womb of earth
Is warmed with secret strength for better birth;
Or, when the latent vice is cured by fire,
Redundant humors through the pores expire;

Or that the warmth distends the chinks, and makes
New breathings, whence new nourishment she takes;
Or that the heat the gaping ground constrains,
New knits the surface, and new strings the veins;
Lest soaking showers should pierce her tender seat.
Or freezing Boreas chill her genial heat,
Or scorching suns too violently beat.
   Nor is the profit small the peasant makes,
Who smooths with harrows, or who pounds with rakes,
The crumbling clods; nor Ceres from on high
Regards his labors with a grudging eye;
Nor his, who ploughs across the furrowed grounds,
And on the back of earth inflicts new wounds;
For he, with frequent exercise, commands
The unwilling soil, and tames the stubborn lands.
   Ye swains, invoke the powers who rule the sky,
For a moist summer, and a winter dry;
For winter drought rewards the peasant's pain,
And broods indulgent on the buried grain.
Hence Mysia boasts her harvests, and the tops
Of Gargarus admire their happy crops.
When first the soil receives the fruitful seed
Make no delay, but cover it with speed:
So fenced from cold, the pliant furrows break,
Before the surly clod resists the rake;
And calls the floods from high, to rush amain
With pregnant streams, to swell the teeming grain.
Then, when the fiery suns too fiercely play,

And shrivelled herbs on withering stems decay,
The wary ploughman, on the mountain's brow,
Undams his watery stores — huge torrents flow,
And, rattling down the rocks, large moisture yield,
Tempering the thirsty fever of the field;
And, lest the stem, too feeble for the freight,
Should scarce sustain the head's unwieldy weight,
Sends in his feeding flocks betimes, to invade
The rising bulk of the luxuriant blade,
Ere yet the aspiring offspring of the grain
O'ertops the ridges of the furrowed plain;
And drains the standing waters, when they yield
Too large a beverage to the drunken field:
But most in autumn, and the showery spring,
When dubious months uncertain weather bring;
When fountains open, when impetuous rain
Swells hasty brooks, and pours upon the plain;
When earth with slime and mud is covered o'er,
Or hollow places spew their watery store.
  Nor yet the ploughman, nor the laboring steer,
Sustain alone the hazards of the year:
But glutton geese, and the Strymonian crane,
With foreign troops invade the tender grain;
And towering weeds malignant shadows yield;
And spreading succory chokes the rising field.
The sire of gods and men, with hard decrees,
Forbids our plenty to be bought with ease,
And wills that mortal men, inured to toil,

Should exercise with pains, the grudging soil;
Himself invented first the shining share,
And whetted human industry by care;
Himself did handicrafts and arts ordain,
Nor suffered sloth to rust his active reign.
Ere this, no peasant vexed the peaceful ground,
Which only turfs and greens for altars, found:
No fences parted fields, nor marks nor bounds
Distinguished acres of litigious grounds;
But all was common, and the fruitful earth
Was free to give her unexacted birth.
Jove added venom to the viper's brood,
And swelled, with raging storms, the peaceful flood;
Commissioned hungry wolves to infest the fold,
And shook from oaken leaves the liquid gold;
Removed from human reach the cheerful fire,
And from the rivers bade the wine retire;
That studious need might useful arts explore;
From furrowed fields to reap the foodful store,
And force the veins of clashing flints to expire
The lurking seeds of their celestial fire.
Then first on seas the hollowed alder swam;
Then sailors quartered heaven, and found a name
For every fixed and every wandering star —
The Pleiads, Hyads, and the Northern Car.
Then toils for beasts, and lime for birds, were found,
And deep-mouthed dogs did forest walks surround;
And casting-nets were spread in shallow brooks,

14

Drags in the deep, and baits were hung on hooks.
Then saws were toothed, and sounding axes made
(For wedges first did yielding wood invade);
And various arts in order did succeed
(What cannot endless labor, urged by need?).

First Ceres taught, the ground with grain to sow,
And armed with iron shares the crooked plough;
When now Dodonian oaks no more supplied
Their mast, and trees their forest-fruit denied.
Soon was his labor doubled to the swain,
And blasting mildews blackened all his grain;
Tough thistles choked the fields, and killed the corn,
And an unthrifty crop of weeds was born:
Then burs and brambles, an unbidden crew
Of graceless guests, the unhappy field subdue;
And oats unblest, and darnel domineers
And shoots his head above the shining ears;
So that, unless the land with daily care
Is exercised, and, with an iron war

Of rakes and harrows, the proud foes expelled,
And birds with clamors frighted from the field —
Unless the boughs are lopped that shade the plain,
And heaven invoked with vows for fruitful rain —
On others' crops you may with envy look,
And shake for food the long-abandoned oak.
  Nor must we pass untold what arms they wield,
Who labor tillage and the furrowed field;
Without whose aid the ground her corn denies,
And nothing can be sown, and nothing rise —
The crooked plough, the share, the towering height
Of waggons, and the cart's unwieldy weight,
The sled, the tumbril, hurdles, and the flail,
The fan of Bacchus, with the flying sail —
These all must be prepared, if ploughmen hope
The promised blessing of a bounteous crop.
Young elms, with early force, in copses bow,
Fit for the figure of the crooked plough.
Of eight feet long a fastened beam prepare
On either side the head, produce an ear;
And sink a socket for the shining share.
Of beech the plough-tail, and the bending yoke,
Or softer linden hardened in the smoke.
I could be long in precepts, but I fear
So mean a subject might offend your ear.
  Delve of convenient depth your thrashing-floor:
With tempered clay then fill and face it o'er;
And let the weighty roller run the round,

To smooth the surface of the unequal ground;
Lest, cracked with summer heats, the flooring flies
Or sinks, and through the crannies weeds arise:
For sundry foes the rural realm surround:
The field-mouse builds her garner under ground
For gathered grain: the blind laborious mole
In winding mazes works her hidden hole:
In hollow caverns vermin make abode —
The hissing serpent, and the swelling toad:
The corn-devouring weasel here abides,
And the wise ant her wintry store provides.
   Mark well the flowering almonds in the wood;
If odorous blooms the bearing branches load,
The glebe will answer to the sylvan reign;
Great heats will follow, and large crops of grain.
But, if a wood of leaves o'ershade the tree,
Such and so barren will thy harvest be:
In vain the hind shall vex the thrashing-floor;
For empty chaff and straw will be thy store.
Some steep their seed, and some in cauldrons boil
With vigorous nitre and with lees of oil,
O'er gentle fires, the exuberant juice to drain,
And swell the flattering husks with fruitful grain.
Yet is not the success for years assured,
Though chosen is the seed, and fully cured,
Unless the peasant, with his annual pain,
Renews his choice, and culls the largest grain.
Thus all below, whether by Nature's curse,

Or Fate's decree, degenerate still to worse.
So the boat's brawny crew the current stem,
And, slow advancing, struggle with the stream:
But if they slack their hands, or cease to strive,
Then down the flood with headlong haste they drive.
   Nor must the ploughman less observe the skies,
When the Kids, Dragon, and Arcturus, rise,
Than sailors homeward bent, who cut their way
Through Helle's stormy straits, and oyster-breeding sea.
But, when Astæa's Balance hung on high,
Betwixt the nights and days divides the sky,
Then yoke your oxen, sow your winter-grain,
Till cold December comes with driving rain.
Linseed and fruitful poppy bury warm,
In a dry season, and prevent the storm.
Sow beans and clover in a rotten soil,
And millet rising from your annual toil,
When with his golden horns, in full career,
The Bull beats down the barriers of the year,
And Argo and the Dog forsake the northern sphere.
   But, if your care to wheat alone extend,
Let Maia with her sisters first descend,
And the bright Gnossian diadem downward bend,
Before you trust in earth your future hope;
Or else expect a listless lazy crop.
Some swains have sown before; but most have found
A husky harvest from the grudging ground.
Vile vetches would you sow, or lentils lean?

The growth of Egypt, or the kidney-bean,
Begin when the slow Waggoner descends;
Nor cease your sowing till mid-winter ends.
For this, through twelve bright signs Apollo guides
The year, and earth in several climes divides.
Five girdles bind the skies: the torrid zone
Glows with the passing and repassing sun:
Far on the right and left, the extremes of heaven
To frosts and snows and bitter blasts are given;
Betwixt the midst and these, the gods assigned
Two habitable seats for human kind,
And, 'cross their limits, cut a sloping way,
Which the twelve signs in beauteous order sway.
Two poles turn round the globe; one seen to rise
O'er Scythian hills, and one in Libyan skies;
The first sublime in heaven, the last is whirled
Below the regions of the nether world.
　　Around our pole the spiry Dragon glides,
And, like a winding stream, the Bears divides —
The less and greater, who by Fate's decree,
Abhor to dive beneath the northern sea.
There, as they say, perpetual night is found
In silence brooding on the unhappy ground:
Or, when Aurora leaves our northern sphere,
She lights the downward heaven, and rises there
And, when on us she breathes the living light,
Red Vesper kindles there the tapers of the night.
From hence uncertain seasons we may know,

19

And when to reap the grain, and when to sow
Or when to fell the furzes; when 'tis meet
To spread the flying canvas for the fleet.
Observe what stars arise or disappear;
And the four quarters of the rolling year.
But, when cold weather and continued rain
The laboring husband in his house restrain,
Let him forecast his work with timely care,
Which else is huddled, when the skies are fair:
Then let him mark the sheep, or whet the shining share,
Or hollow trees for boats, or number o'er
His sacks, or measure his increasing store,
Or sharpen stakes, or head the forks, or twine
The sallow twigs to tie the straggling vine;
Or wicker baskets weave, or air the corn,
Or grinded grain betwixt two marbles turn.
No laws, divine or human, can restrain
From necessary works the laboring swain,
E'en holidays and feasts permission yield
To float the meadows, or to fence the field,
To fire the brambles, snare the birds, and steep
In wholesome water-falls the woolly sheep.
And oft the drudging ass is driven with toil,
To neighboring towns with apples and with oil;
Returning, late and laden, home with gain
Of bartered pitch, and hand-mills for the grain.
   The lucky days, in each revolving moon,
For labor choose; the fifth be sure to shun;

That gave the Furies and pale Pluto birth,
And armed, against the skies, the sons of earth.
With mountains piled on mountains, thrice they strove
To scale the steepy battlements of Jove;
And thrice his lightning and red thunder played,
And their demolished works in ruin laid.
The seventh is, next the tenth, the best to join
Young oxen to the yoke, and plant the vine.
Then, weavers, stretch your stays upon the weft:
The ninth is good for travel, bad for theft.
Some works in dead of night are better done,
Or when the morning dew prevents the sun.
Parched meads and stubble, mow by Phœbe's light,
Which both require the coolness of the night;
For moisture then abounds, and pearly rains
Descend in silence to refresh the plains.
The wife and husband equally conspire
To work by night, and rake the winter fire:
He sharpens torches in the glimmering room;
She shoots the flying shuttle through the loom;
Or boils in kettles must of wine, and skims
With leaves, the dregs that overflow the brims:
And till the watchful cock awakes the day,
She sings, to drive the tedious hours away.
But, in warm weather, when the skies are clear,
By daylight reap the product of the year;
And in the sun your golden grain display,
And thrash it out, and winnow it by day.

Plough naked, swain, and naked sow the land;
For lazy winter numbs the laboring hand.
In genial winter, swains enjoy their store,
Forget their hardships, and recruit for more.
The farmer to full bowls invites his friends,
And, what he got with pains, with pleasure spends.
So sailors, when escaped from stormy seas,
First crown their vessels, then indulge their ease.
Yet that's the proper time to thrash the wood
For mast of oak, your fathers' homely food;
To gather laurel-berries, and the spoil
Of bloody myrtles, and to press your oil;
For stalking cranes to set the guileful snare;
To inclose the stags in toils, and hunt the hare;
With Balearic slings, or Gnossian bow,
To persecute from far the flying doe,
Then, when the fleecy skies new-clothe the wood,
And cakes of rustling ice come rolling down the flood.

   Now sing we stormy stars, when autumn weighs
The year, and adds to nights, and shortens days,
And suns declining shine with feeble rays;
What cares must then attend the toiling swain;
Or when the lowering spring, with lavish rain,
Beats down the slender stem and bearded grain,
While yet the head is green, or, lightly swelled
With milky moisture, overlooks the field.
E'en when the farmer, now secure of fear,
Sends in the swains to spoil the finished year,

E'en while the reaper fills his greedy hands,
And binds the golden sheaves in brittle bands,
Oft have I seen a sudden storm arise,
From all the warring winds that sweep the skies:
The heavy harvest from the root is torn,
And whirled aloft, the lighter stubble borne:
With such a force the flying rack is driven,
And such a winter wears the face of heaven:
And oft whole sheets descend of sluicy rain,
Sucked by the spongy clouds from off the main:
The lofty skies at once come pouring down,
The promised crop and golden labors drown.
The dikes are filled; and, with a roaring sound,
The rising rivers float the nether ground;
And rocks the bellowing voice of boiling seas rebound.
The father of the gods his glory shrouds,
Involved in tempests, and a night of clouds;
And from the middle darkness flashing out,
By fits he deals his fiery bolts about.
Earth feels the motions of her angry god:
Her entrails tremble, and her mountains nod,
And flying beasts in forests seek abode:
Deep horror seizes every human breast;
Their pride is humbled and their fear confessed,
While he from high his rolling thunder throws,
And fires the mountains with repeated blows:
The rocks are from their old foundation rent;
The winds redouble, and the rains augment:

The waves on heaps are dashed against the shore;
And now the woods, and now the billows, roar.
   In fear of this, observe the starry signs,
Where Saturn houses, and where Hermes joins.
But first to heaven thy due devotions pay,
And annual gifts on Ceres' altars lay.
When winter's rage abates, when cheerful hours
Awake the spring, the spring awakes the flowers,
On the green turf thy careless limbs display,
And celebrate the mighty Mother's day;
For then the hills with pleasing shades are crowned,
And sleeps are sweeter on the silken ground.
With milder beams the sun securely shines;
Fat are the lambs, and luscious are the wines.
Let every swain adore her power divine,
And milk and honey mix with sparkling wine;
Let all the choir of clowns attend the show,
In long procession, shouting as they go;
Invoking her to bless their yearly stores,
Inviting plenty to their crowded floors.
Thus in the spring, and thus in summer's heat,
Before the sickles touch the ripening wheat,
On Ceres call; and let the laboring hind
With oaken wreaths his hollow temples bind:
On Ceres let him call, and Ceres praise,
With uncouth dances, and with country lays.
   And that by certain signs we may presage
Of heats and rains, and winds' impetuous rage,

The sovereign of the heavens has set on high
The moon to mark the changes of the sky;
When southern blasts should cease, and when the swain
Should near their folds his feeding flocks restrain.
For, ere the rising winds begin to roar,
The working seas advance to wash the shore;
Soft whispers run along the leafy woods,
And mountains whistle to the murmuring floods.
E'en then the doubtful billows scarce abstain
From the tossed vessel on the troubled main;
When crying cormorants forsake the sea,
And, stretching to the covert, wing their way;
When sportful coots run skimming o'er the strand,
When watchful herons leave their watery stand,
And, mounting upward with erected flight,
Gain on the skies, and soar above the sight.
And oft, before tempestuous winds arise,
The seeming stars fall headlong from the skies,
And, shooting through the darkness, gild the night
With sweeping glories, and long trails of light;
And chaff with eddy winds is whirled around,
And dancing leaves are lifted from the ground;
And floating feathers on the waters play.
　　But when the wingèd thunder takes his way
From the cold north, and east and west engage,
And at their frontiers meet with equal rage,
The clouds are crushed; a glut of gathered rain
The hollow ditches fills, and floats the plain;

And sailors furl their drooping sheets amain.
Wet weather seldom hurts the most unwise;
So plain the signs, such prophets are the skies.
The wary crane foresees it first, and sails
Above the storm, and leaves the lowly vales;
The cow looks up, and from afar can find
The change of heaven, and snuffs it in the wind;
The swallow skims the river's watery face;
The frogs renew the croaks of their loquacious race;
The careful ant her secret cell forsakes,
And drags her eggs along the narrow tracks:

At either horn the rainbow drinks the flood;
Huge flocks of rising rooks forsake their food,
And, crying, seek the shelter of the wood.
Besides, the several sorts of watery fowls,
That swim the seas, or haunt the standing pools,
The swans that sail along the silver flood,
And dive with stretching necks to search their food,
Then lave their backs with sprinkling dew in vain,

And stem the stream to meet the promised rain.
The crow with clamorous cries the shower demands,
And single stalks along the desert sands.
The nightly virgin, while her wheel she plies,
Foresees the storm impending in the skies,
When sparkling lamps their sputtering light advance,
And in the sockets oily bubbles dance.
  Then, after showers, 'tis easy to descry
Returning suns, and a serener sky:
The stars shine smarter; and the moon adorns,
As with unborrowed beams, her sharpened horns.
The filmy gossamer now flits no more,
Nor halcyons bask on the short sunny shore;
Their litter is not tossed by sows unclean;
But a blue droughty mist descends upon the plain;
And owls, that mark the setting sun, declare
A star-light evening, and a morning fair.
Towering aloft, avenging Nisus flies,
While, dared, below the guilty Scylla lies.
Wherever frighted Scylla flies away,
Swift Nisus follows and pursues his prey:
Where injured Nisus takes his airy course,
Thence trembling Scylla flies, and shuns his force:
This punishment pursues the unhappy maid,
And thus the purple hair is dearly paid.
  Then, thrice the ravens rend the liquid air,
And croaking notes proclaim the settled fair.
Then round their airy palaces they fly.

To greet the sun; and seized with secret joy,
When storms are overblown, with food repair
To their forsaken nests and callow care.
Not that I think their breasts with heavenly souls
Inspired, as man, who destiny controls:
But, with the changeful temper of the skies,
As rains condense, and sunshine rarefies,
So turn the species in their altered minds,
Composed by calms, and discomposed by winds.
From hence proceeds the birds' harmonious voice;
From hence the cows exult, and frisking lambs rejoice.
   Observe the daily circle of the sun,
And the short year of each revolving moon:
By them thou shalt foresee the following day,
Nor shall a starry night thy hopes betray.
When first the moon appears, if then she shrouds
Her silver crescent tipped with sable clouds,
Conclude she bodes a tempest on the main,
And brews for fields impetuous floods of rain.
Or, if her face with fiery flushing glow,
Expect the rattling winds aloft to blow.
But, four nights old (for that's the surest sign),
With sharpened horns if glorious then she shine,
Next day, not only that, but all the moon,
Till her revolving race be wholly run,
Are void of tempests, both by land and sea;
And sailors in the port their promised vow shall pay.
   Above the rest, the sun, who never lies,

Foretells the change of weather in the skies:
For, if he rise unwilling to his race,
Clouds on his brow, and spots upon his face:
Or if through mists he shoots his sullen beams,
Frugal of light, in loose and straggling streams;
Suspect a drizzling day, with southern rain,
Fatal to fruits, and flocks, and promised grain.
Or if Aurora, with half-opened eyes,
And a pale sickly cheek, salute the skies;
How shall the vine, with tender leaves, defend
Her teeming clusters, when the storms descend,
When ridgy roofs and tiles can scarce avail
To bar the ruin of the rattling hail?
  But, more than all, the setting sun survey,
When down the steep of heaven he drives the day:
For oft we find him finishing his race,
With various colors erring on his face.
If fiery red his glowing globe descends,
High winds and furious tempests he portends:
But, if his cheeks are swoln with livid blue,
He bodes wet weather by his watery hue:
If dusky spots are varied on his brow,
And, streaked with red, a troubled color show;
That sullen mixture shall at once declare
Winds, rain, and storms, and elemental war.
What desperate madman then would venture o'er
The frith, or haul his cables from the shore?
But, if with purple rays he brings the light,

And a pure heaven resigns to quiet night,
No rising winds, or falling storms are nigh;
But northern breezes through the forests fly,
And drive the rack, and purge the ruffled sky.
The unerring sun by certain signs declares,
What the late e'en or early morn prepares,
And when the south projects a stormy day,
And when the clearing north will puff the clouds away.
  The sun reveals the secrets of the sky;
And who dares give the source of light the lie?
The change of empires often he declares,
Fierce tumults, hidden treasons, open wars.
He first the fate of Cæsar did foretell,
And pitied Rome, when Rome in Cæsar fell;
In iron clouds concealed the public light;
And impious mortals feared eternal night.
  Nor was the fact foretold by him alone:
Nature herself stood forth, and seconded the sun.
Earth, air, and seas, with prodigies were signed;
And birds obscene, and howling dogs, divined.
What rocks did Ætna's bellowing mouth expire
From her torn entrails! and what floods of fire!
What clanks were heard, in German skies afar,
Of arms, and armies, rushing to the war!
Dire earthquakes rent the solid Alps below,
And from their summits shook the eternal snow!
Pale spectres in the close of night were seen,
And voices heard, of more than mortal men,

In silent groves: dumb sheep and oxen spoke;
And streams ran backward, and their beds forsook;
The yawning earth disclosed the abyss of hell:
The weeping statues did the wars foretell;
And holy sweat from brazen idols fell.
Then, rising in his might, the king of floods
Rushed through the forests, tore the lofty woods,
And, rolling onward, with a sweepy sway,
Bore houses, herds, and laboring hinds away.
Blood sprang from wells; wolves howled in towns by night,
And boding victims did the priests affright.
Such peals of thunder never poured from high,
Nor forky lightnings flashed from such a sullen sky.
Red meteors ran across the ethereal space;
Stars disappeared, and comets took their place.
For this, the Emathian plains once more were strewed
With Roman bodies, and just heaven thought good
To fatten twice those fields with Roman blood.
Then, after length of time, the laboring swains
Who turn the turfs of those unhappy plains,
Shall rusty piles from the ploughed furrows take,
And over empty helmets pass the rake —
Amazed at antique titles on the stones,
And mighty relics of gigantic bones.
   Ye home-born deities, of mortal birth!
Thou father Romulus, and mother Earth,
Goddess unmoved! whose guardian arms extend
O'er Tuscan Tiber's course, and Roman towers defend;

With youthful Cæsar your joint powers engage,
Nor hinder him to save the sinking age.
O! let the blood, already spilt, atone
For the past crimes of cursed Laomedon!
Heaven wants thee there; and long the gods, we know,
Have grudged thee, Cæsar, to the world below,
Where fraud and rapine right and wrong confound,
Where impious arms from every part resound,
And monstrous crimes in every shape are crowned.
The peaceful peasant to the wars is pressed;
The fields lie fallow in inglorious rest;
The plain no pasture to the flock affords;
The crooked scythes are straightened into swords:
And there Euphrates her soft offspring arms,
And here the Rhine rebellows with alarms;
The neighboring cities range on several sides;
Perfidious Mars long-plighted leagues divides,
And o'er the wasted world in triumph rides.
So four fierce coursers, starting to the race,
Scour through the plain, and lengthen every pace;
Nor reins, nor curbs, nor threatening cries, they fear,
But force along the trembling charioteer.

THE SECOND GEORGIC

THE ARGUMENT

*The subject of the following book is planting: in handling of
which argument, the poet shews all the different methods of
raising trees, describes their variety, and gives rules for the
management of each in particular. He then points out the soils
in which the several plants thrive best, and thence takes occa-
sion to run out into the praises of Italy; after which, he gives
some directions for discovering the nature of every soil, pre-
scribes rules for dressing of vines, olives, &c., and
concludes the Georgic with a panegyric
on a country life.*

Thus far of tillage, and of heavenly signs:
Now sing, my muse, the growth of generous vines.
The shady groves, the woodland progeny,
And the slow product of Minerva's tree.
Great father Bacchus! to my song repair;
For clustering grapes are thy peculiar care:
For thee, large bunches load the bending vine;
And the last blessings of the year are thine.
To thee his joys the jolly Autumn owes,
When the fermenting juice the vat o'erflows.
Come, strip with me, my god! come drench all o'er
Thy limbs in must of wine, and drink at every pore.
Some trees their birth to bounteous Nature owe;
For some, without the pains of planting, grow.
With osiers thus the banks of brooks abound,
Sprung from the watery genius of the ground.
From the same principles gray willows come,
Herculean poplar, and the tender broom.
But some, from seeds inclosed in earth, arise;

For thus the mastful chestnut mates the skies.
Hence rise the branching beech and vocal oak,
Where Jove of old oraculously spoke.
Some from the root a rising wood disclose:
Thus elms, and thus the savage cherry grows:
Thus the green bay, that binds the poet's brows,
Shoots, and is sheltered by the mother's boughs.
    These ways of planting, Nature did ordain
For trees and shrubs, and all the sylvan reign.
Others there are, by late experience found:
Some cut the shoots, and plant in furrowed ground;
Some cover rooted stalks in deeper mould;
Some, cloven stakes; and (wondrous to behold!)
Their sharpened ends in earth their footing place;
And the dry poles produce a living race.
Some bow their vines, which buried in the plain,
Their tops in distant arches rise again.
Others no root require; the laborer cuts
Young slips, and in the soil securely puts.
E'en stumps of olives, bared of leaves, and dead,
Revive, and oft redeem their withered head.
'Tis usual now an inmate graff to see
With insolence invade a foreign tree:
Thus pears and quinces from the crab-tree come
And thus the ruddy cornel bears the plum.
    Then let the learnèd gardener mark with care
The kinds of stocks, and what those kinds will bear;
Explore the nature of each several tree,

And, known, improve with artful industry:
And let no spot of idle earth be found,
But cultivate the genius of the ground:
For open Ismarus will Bacchus please;
Taburnus loves the shade of olive-trees.

 The virtues of the several soils I sing. —
Mæcenas, now thy needful succor bring!
O thou! the better part of my renown,
Inspire thy poet, and thy poem crown:
Embark with me, while I new tracts explore,
With flying sails and breezes from the shore:
Not that my song, in such a scanty space,
So large a subject fully can embrace —
Not though I were supplied with iron lungs,
A hundred mouths, filled with as many tongues:
But steer my vessel with a steady hand,
And coast along the shore in sight of land.
Nor will I tire thy patience with a train
Of preface, or what ancient poets feign.

 The trees, which of themselves advance in air,
Are barren kinds, but strongly built and fair,
Because the vigor of the native earth
Maintains the plant, and makes a manly birth.
Yet these, receiving graffs of other kind,
Or thence transplanted, change their savage mind,
Their wildness lose, and, quitting nature's part,
Obey the rules and discipline of art.
The same do trees, that, sprung from barren roots,

41

In open fields transplanted bear their fruits.
For, where they grow, the native energy
Turns all into the substance of the tree,
Starves and destroys the fruit, is only made
For brawny bulk, and for a barren shade.
The plant that shoots from seed, a sullen tree,
At leisure grows, for late posterity;
The generous flavor lost, the fruits decay,
And savage grapes are made the birds' ignoble prey.
    Much labor is required in trees, to tame
Their wild disorder, and in ranks reclaim.
Well must the ground be digged, and better dressed,
New soil to make, and meliorate the rest.
Old stakes of olive trees in plants revive;
By the same method Paphian myrtles live;
But nobler vines by propagation thrive.
From roots hard hazels, and, from scions, rise
Tall ash, and taller oak that mates the skies;
Palm, poplar, fir, descending from the steep
Of hills, to try the dangers of the deep.
The thin-leaved arbute, hazel-graffs receives;
And planes huge apples bear, that bore but leaves.
Thus mastful beech the bristly chestnut bears,
And the wild ash is white with blooming pears,
And greedy swine, from grafted elms are fed
With falling acorns, that on oaks are bred.
    But various are the ways to change the state
Of plants, to bud, to graff, to inoculate.

42

For, where the tender rinds of trees disclose
Their shooting gems, a swelling knot there grows:
Just in that space a narrow slit we make,
Then other buds from bearing trees we take;
Inserted thus, the wounded rind we close,
In whose moist womb the admitted infant grows.
But, when the smoother bole from knots is free,
We make a deep incision in the tree,
And in the solid wood the slip inclose;

The battening bastard shoots again and grows;
And in short space the laden boughs arise,
With happy fruit advancing to the skies.
The mother plant admires the leaves unknown
Of alien trees, and apples not her own.
   Of vegetable woods are various kinds,
And the same species are of several minds.
Lotes, willows, elms, have different forms allowed;
So funeral cypress, rising like a shroud.
Fat olive-trees of sundry sorts appear,

43

Of sundry shapes their unctuous berries bear.
Radii long olives, Orchites round produce,
And bitter Pausia, pounded for the juice.
Alcinous' orchard various apples bears:
Unlike are bergamots and pounder pears.
Nor our Italian vines produce the shape,
Or taste, or flavor, of the Lesbian grape.
The Thasian vines in richer soils abound;
The Mareotic grow in barren ground.
The Psythian grape we dry: Lagean juice
Will stammering tongues and staggering feet produce.
Rath ripe are some, and some of later kind;
Of golden some, and some of purple rind.
How shall I praise the Rhætian grape divine,
Which yet contends not with Falernian wine?
The Aminean many a consulship survives,
And longer than the Lydian vintage lives,
Or high Phanæus, king of Chian growth:
But, for large quantities and lasting, both,
The less Argitis bears the prize away.
The Rhodian, sacred to the solemn day,
In second services is poured to Jove,
And best accepted by the gods above.
Nor must Bumastus his old honors lose,
In length and largeness like the dugs of cows.
I pass the rest, whose every race, and name,
And kinds, are less material to my theme;
Which who would learn, as soon may tell the sands,

Driven by the western wind on Libyan lands,
Or number, when the blustering Eurus roars,
The billows beating on Ionian shores.
   Nor every plant on every soil will grow:
The sallow loves the watery ground, and low;
The marshes, alders: Nature seems to ordain
The rocky cliff for the wild ash's reign;
The baleful yew to northern blasts assigns,
To shores the myrtles, and to mounts the vines.
   Regard the extremest cultivated coast,
From hot Arabia to the Scythian frost:
All sorts of trees their several countries know;
Black ebon only will in India grow,
And odorous frankincense on the Sabæan bough.
Balm slowly trickles through the bleeding veins
Of happy shrubs in Idumæan plains.
The green Egyptian thorn, for med'cine good,
With Æthiops' hoary trees and woolly wood,
Let others tell; and how the Seres spin
Their fleecy forests in a slender twine;
With mighty trunks of trees on Indian shores,
Whose height above the feathered arrow soars,
Shot from the toughest bow, and, by the brawn
Of expert archers, with vast vigor drawn.
Sharp-tasted citrons, Median climes produce
(Bitter the rind, but generous is the juice),
A cordial fruit, a present antidote
Against the direful stepdame's deadly draught,

Who, mixing wicked weeds with words impure,
The fate of envied orphans would procure.
Large is the plant, and like a laurel grows,
And, did it not a different scent disclose,
A laurel were: the fragrant flowers contemn
The stormy winds, tenacious of their stem.
With this, the Medes to laboring age bequeath
New lungs, and cure the sourness of the breath.
    But neither Median woods (a plenteous land),
Fair Ganges, Hermus rolling golden sand,
Nor Bactria, nor the richer Indian fields,
Nor all the gummy stores Arabia yields,
Nor any foreign earth of greater name,
Can with sweet Italy contend in fame.
No bulls, whose nostrils breathe a living flame,
Have turned our turf; no teeth of serpents here
Were sown, an armèd host and iron crop to bear.
But fruitful vines, and the fat olive's freight,
And harvests heavy with their fruitful weight,
Adorn our fields; and on the cheerful green
The grazing flocks and lowing herds are seen.
The warrior horse, here bred, is taught to train:
There flows Clitumnus through the flowery plain,
Whose waves, for triumphs after prosperous war,
The victim ox and snowy sheep prepare.
Perpetual spring our happy climate sees:
Twice breed the cattle, and twice bear the trees;
And summer suns recede by slow degrees.

Our land is from the rage of tigers freed,
Nor nourishes the lion's angry seed;
Nor poisonous aconite is here produced,
Or grows unknown, or is, when known, refused;
Nor in so vast a length our serpents glide,
Or raised on such a spiry volume ride.
  Next add our cities of illustrious name,
Their costly labor, and stupendous frame;
Our forts on steepy hills, that far below
See wanton streams in winding valleys flow;
Our twofold seas, that, washing either side,
A rich recruit of foreign stores provide;
Our spacious lakes; thee, Larius, first; and next
Benacus, with tempestuous billows vexed.
Or shall I praise thy ports, or mention make
Of the vast mound that binds the Lucrine lake?
Or the disdainful sea, that, shut from thence,
Roars round the structure, and invades the fence,
There, where secure the Julian waters glide,
Or where Avernus' jaws admit the Tyrrhene tide?
Our quarries, deep in earth, were famed of old
For veins of silver, and for ore of gold.
The inhabitants themselves their country grace,
Hence rose the Marsian and Sabellian race,
Strong-limbed and stout, and to the wars inclined,
And hard Ligurians a laborious kind,
And Volscians armed with iron-headed darts.
Besides — an offspring of undaunted hearts —

47

The Decii, Marii, great Camillus, came
From hence, and greater Scipio's double name,
And mighty Cæsar, whose victorious arms
To farthest Asia carry fierce alarms,
Avert unwarlike Indians from his Rome,
Triumph abroad, secure our peace at home.
　　Hail, sweet Saturnian soil! of fruitful grain
Great parent, greater of illustrious men!
For thee my tuneful accents will I raise,
And treat of arts disclosed in ancient days,
Once more unlocked for thee the sacred spring,
And old Ascræan verse in Roman cities sing.
　　The nature of the several soils now see,
Their strength, their color, their fertility:
And first for heath, and barren hilly ground,
Where meagre clay and flinty stones abound,
Where the poor soil all succor seems to want —
Yet this suffices the Palladian plant.
Undoubted signs of such a soil are found;
For here wild olive-shoots o'erspread the ground,
And heaps of berries strew the fields around.
But, where the soil, with fattening moisture filled,
Is clothed with grass, and fruitful to be tilled,
Such as in cheerful vales we view from high,
Which dripping rocks with rolling streams supply,
And feed with ooze; where rising hillocks run
In length, and open to the southern sun;
Where fern succeeds, ungrateful to the plough —

That gentle ground to generous grapes allow.
Strong stocks of vines it will in time produce,
And overflow the vats with friendly juice,
Such as our priests in golden goblets pour
To gods, the givers of the cheerful hour,
Then when the bloated Tuscan blows his horn,
And reeking entrails are in chargers borne.
  If herds or fleecy flocks be more thy care,
Or goats that graze the field, and burn it bare,
Then seek Tarentum's lawns, and farthest coast,
Or such a field as hapless Mantua lost,
Where silver swans sail down the watery road,
And graze the floating herbage of the flood.
There crystal streams perpetual tenor keep,
Nor food nor springs are wanting to thy sheep;
For, what the day devours, the nightly dew
Shall to the morn in pearly drops renew.
Fat crumbling earth is fitter for the plough,
Putrid and loose above, and black below;
For ploughing is an imitative toil,
Resembling nature in an easy soil.
No land for seed like this; no fields afford
So large an income to the village lord:
No toiling teams from harvest-labor come
So late at night, so heavy-laden home.
The like of forest land is understood,
From whence the surly ploughman grubs the wood,
Which had for length of ages idly stood.

Then birds forsake the ruins of their seat,
And, flying from their nests, their callow young forget.
The coarse lean gravel, on the mountain-sides,
Scarce dewy beverage for the bees provides;
Nor chalk, nor crumbling stones, the food of snakes,
That work in hollow earth their winding tracks.
The soil exhaling clouds of subtle dews,
Imbibing moisture which with ease she spews,
Which rusts not iron, and whose mould is clean,
Well clothed with cheerful grass, and ever green,
Is good for olives, and aspiring vines,
Embracing husband elms in amorous twines;
Is fit for feeding cattle, fit to sow,
And equal to the pasture and the plough.
Such is the soil of fat Campanian fields;
Such large increase the land that joins Vesuvius yields;
And such a country could Acerræ boast,
Till Clanius overflowed the unhappy coast.
    I teach thee next the differing soils to know,
The light for vines, the heavier for the plough.
Choose first a place for such a purpose fit;
There dig the solid earth, and sink a pit;
Next fill the hole with its own earth again,
And trample with thy feet, and tread it in:
Then, if it rise not to the former height
Of superfice, conclude that soil is light,
A proper ground for pasturage and vines.
But if the sullen earth, so pressed, repines

Within its native mansion to retire,
And stays without, a heap of heavy mire,
'Tis good for arable, a glebe that asks
Tough teams of oxen, and laborious tasks.
　　Salt earth and bitter are not fit to sow,
Nor will be tamed and mended by the plough.
Sweet grapes degenerate there; and fruits declined
From their first flavorous taste, renounce their kind.
This truth by sure experiment is tried;
For first an osier colander provide
Of twigs thick wrought (such, toiling peasants twine,
When through strait passages they strain their wine):
In this close vessel place that earth accursed,
But filled brimful with wholesome water first;
Then run it through: the drops will rope around,
And, by the bitter taste, disclose the ground.
The fatter earth by handling we may find,
With ease distinguished from the meagre kind:
Poor soil will crumble into dust; the rich
Will to the fingers cleave like clammy pitch:
Moist earth produces corn and grass, but both
Too rank and too luxuriant in their growth.
Let not my land so large a promise boast,
Lest the lank ears in length of stem be lost.
The heavier earth is by her weight betrayed;
The lighter in the poising hand is weighed.
'Tis easy to distinguish by the sight,
The color of the soil, and black from white.

But the cold ground is difficult to know;
Yet this, the plants that prosper there, will show —
Black ivy, pitch-trees, and the baleful yew.
   These rules considered well, with early care
The vineyard destined for thy vines prepare:
But long before the planting, dig the ground,
With furrows deep that cast a rising mound.
The clods, exposed to winter winds, will bake;
For putrid earth will best in vineyards take;
And hoary frosts, after the painful toil
Of delving hinds, will rot the mellow soil.
   Some peasants, not to omit the nicest care,
Of the same soil their nursery prepare,
With that of their plantation; lest the tree,
Translated, should not with the soil agree.
Beside, to plant it as it was, they mark
The heaven's four quarters on the tender bark,
And to the north or south, restore the side,
Which at their birth did heat or cold abide:
So strong is custom; such effects can use
In tender souls of pliant plants produce.
   Choose next a province for thy vineyard's reign,
On hills above, or in the lowly plain.
If fertile fields or valleys be thy choice,
Plant thick; for bounteous Bacchus will rejoice
In close plantations there; but, if the vine
On rising ground be placed, or hills supine,
Extend thy loose battalions largely wide,

Opening thy ranks and files on either side,
But marshalled all in order as they stand;
And let no soldier straggle from his band.
As legions in the field their front display,
To try the fortune of some doubtful day,
And move to meet their foes with sober pace,
Strict to their figure, though in wider space,
Before the battle joins, while from afar
The field yet glitters with the pomp of war,
And equal Mars, like an impartial lord,
Leaves all to fortune, and the dint of sword:
So let thy vines in intervals be set,
But not their rural discipline forget;
Indulge their width, and add a roomy space,
That their extremest lines may scarce embrace:
Nor this alone to indulge a vain delight,
And make a pleasing prospect for the sight,
But for the ground itself; this only way
Can equal vigor to the plants convey,
Which, crowded, want the room, their branches to display.
   How deep they must be planted, wouldst thou know?
In shallow furrows vines securely grow.
Not so the rest of plants; for Jove's own tree,
That holds the woods in awful sovereignty,
Requires a depth of lodging in the ground,
And, next the lower skies, a bed profound:
High as the topmost boughs to heaven ascend,
So low his roots to hell's dominion tend.

55

Therefore, nor winds, nor winter's rage, o'erthrows
His bulky body, but unmoved he grows;
For length of ages lasts his happy reign,
And lives of mortal man contend in vain.
Full in the midst of his own strength he stands,
Stretching his brawny arms, and leafy hands:
His shade protects the plains, his head the hills commands.
   The hurtful hazel in thy vineyard shun;
Nor plant it to receive the setting sun;
Nor break the topmost branches from the tree;
Nor prune, with blunted knife, the progeny.
Root up wild olives from thy labored lands;
For sparkling fire, from hinds' unwary hands,
Is often scattered o'er their unctuous rinds,
And after spread abroad by raging winds:
For first the smouldering flame the trunk receives;
Ascending thence, it crackles in the leaves;
At length victorious to the top aspires,
Involving all the wood in smoky fires;
But most, when driven by winds, the flaming storm
Of the long files destroys the beauteous form.
In ashes then the unhappy vineyard lies;
Nor will the blasted plants from ruin rise;
Nor will the withered stock be green again;
But the wild olive shoots, and shades the ungrateful plain.
Be not seduced with wisdom's empty shows,
To stir the peaceful ground when Boreas blows.
When winter frosts constrain the fields with cold,

The fainty root can take no steady hold.
But when the golden spring reveals the year,
And the white bird returns, whom serpents fear,
That season deem the best to plant thy vines:
Next that, is when autumnal warmth declines,
Ere heat is quite decayed, or cold begun,
Or Capricorn admits the winter sun.
  The spring adorns the woods, renews the leaves;
The womb of earth the genial seed receives:
For then almighty Jove descends, and pours
Into his buxom bride his fruitful showers;
And, mixing his large limbs with hers, he feeds
Her births with kindly juice, and fosters teeming seeds.
Then joyous birds frequent the lonely grove,
And beasts, by nature stung, renew their love.
Then fields the blades of buried corn disclose;
And, while the balmy western spirit blows,
Earth to the breath her bosom dares expose.
With kindly moisture then the plants abound;
The grass securely springs above the ground;
The tender twig shoots upward to the skies,
And on the faith of the new sun relies.
The swerving vines on the tall elms prevail;
Unhurt by southern showers, or northern hail,
They spread their gems, the genial warmth to share,
And boldly trust their buds in open air.
  In this soft season (let me dare to sing),
The world was hatched by heaven's imperial king —

In prime of all the year, and holidays of spring.
Then did the new creation first appear;
Nor other was the tenor of the year,
When laughing heaven did the great birth attend;
And eastern winds their wintry breath suspend:
Then sheep first saw the sun in open fields;
And savage beasts were sent to stock the wilds;
And golden stars flew up to light the skies;
And man's relentless race from stony quarries rise.
Nor could the tender new creation bear
The excessive heats or coldness of the year,
But, chilled by winter, or by summer fired,
The middle temper of the spring required,
When warmth and moisture did at once abound,
And heaven's indulgence brooded on the ground.
  For what remains, in depth of earth secure
Thy covered plants, and dung with hot manure;
And shells and gravel in the ground inclose;
For through their hollow chinks the water flows,
Which, thus imbibed, returns in misty dews,
And, steaming up, the rising plant renews.
Some husbandmen, of late, have found the way,
A hilly heap of stones above to lay,
And press the plants with shards of potters' clay.
This fence against immoderate rain they found,
Or when the dog-star cleaves the thirsty ground.
  Be mindful, when thou hast entombed the shoot:
With store of earth around to feed the root;

With iron teeth of rakes and prongs, to move
The crusted earth, and loosen it above.
Then exercise thy sturdy steers to plough
Betwixt thy vines, and teach the feeble row
To mount on reeds, and wands, and, upward led,
On ashen poles to raise their forky head.
On these new crutches let them learn to walk,
Till, swerving upwards with a stronger stalk,
They brave the winds, and, clinging to their guide,
On tops of elms at length triumphant ride.
But, in their tender nonage, while they spread
Their springing leaves, and lift their infant head,
And upward while they shoot in open air,
Indulge their childhood, and the nurselings spare,
Nor exercise thy rage on new-born life;
But let thy hand supply the pruning-knife,
And crop luxuriant stragglers, nor be loth
To strip the branches of their leafy growth.
But, when the rooted vines, with steady hold,
Can clasp their elms, then, husbandman, be bold
To lop the disobedient boughs, that strayed
Beyond their ranks; let crooked steel invade
The lawless troops, which discipline disclaim,
And their superfluous growth with rigor tame.
   Next, fenced with hedges and deep ditches round,
Exclude the encroaching cattle from thy ground,
While yet the tender germs but just appear,
Unable to sustain the uncertain year,

Whose leaves are not alone foul winter's prey,
But oft by summer suns are scorched away;
And, worse than both, become the unworthy browse
Of buffaloes, salt goats, and hungry cows.
For not December's frost, that burns the boughs,
Nor dog-days' parching heat, that splits the rocks,
Are half so harmful as the greedy flocks,
Their venomed bite, and scars indented on the stocks.
For this, the malefactor goat was laid
On Bacchus' altar, and his forfeit paid.
    At Athens thus old comedy began,
When round the streets the reeling actors ran,
In country villages, and crossing ways,
Contending for the prizes of their plays;
And, glad with Bacchus, on the grassy soil,
Leaped o'er the skins of goats besmeared with oil.
Thus Roman youth, derived from ruined Troy,
In rude Saturnian rhymes express their joy;
With taunts, and laughter loud, their audience please,
Deformed with vizards, cut from barks of trees:
In jolly hymns they praise the god of wine,
Whose earthen images adorn the pine,
And there are hung on high, in honor of the vine.
A madness so devout the vineyard fills;
In hollow valleys and on rising hills,
On whate'er side he turns his honest face,
And dances in the wind, those fields are in his grace.
To Bacchus therefor let us tune our lays,

And in our mother-tongue resound his praise.
Thin cakes in chargers, and a guilty goat,
Dragged by the horns, be to his altars brought;
Whose offered entrails shall his crimes reproach,
And drip their fatness from the hazel broach.
  To dress thy vines, new labor is required;
Nor must the painful husbandman be tired:
For thrice, at least, in compass of the year,

Thy vineyard must employ the sturdy steer
To turn the glebe; besides thy daily pain
To break the clods, and make the surface plain,
To unload the branches, or the leaves to thin,
That suck the vital moisture of the vine.
Thus in a circle runs the peasant's pain,
And the year rolls within itself again.
E'en in the lowest months, when storms have shed
From vines the hairy honors of their head,
Not then the drudging hind his labor ends,
But to the coming year his care extends.

E'en then the naked vine he persecutes;
His pruning-knife at once reforms and cuts.
Be first to dig the ground; be first to burn
The branches lopt; and first the props return
Into thy house, that bore the burdened vines;
But last to reap the vintage of thy wines.
    Twice in the year luxuriant leaves o'ershade
The encumbered vine; rough brambles twice invade.
Hard labor both! Commend the large excess
Of spacious vineyards; cultivate the less.
Besides, in woods the shrubs of prickly thorn,
Sallows and reeds on banks of rivers born,
Remain to cut; for vineyards, useful found
To stay thy vines, and fence thy fruitful ground.
Nor when thy tender trees at length are bound;
When peaceful vines from pruning-hooks are free,
When husbands have surveyed the last degree,
And utmost files of plants, and ordered every tree;
E'en when they sing at ease in full content,
Insulting o'er the toils they underwent;
Yet still they find a future task remain,
To turn the soil, and break the clods again;
And, after all, their joys are insincere,
While falling rain on ripening grapes they fear.
Quite opposite to these are olives found:
No dressing they require, and dread no wound,
Nor rakes nor harrows need; but, fixed below,
Rejoice in open air, and unconcern'dly grow.

The soil itself due nourishment supplies:
Plough but the furrows, and the fruits arise,
Content with small endeavors, till they spring.
Soft peace they figure, and sweet plenty bring:
Then olives plant, and hymns to Pallas sing.

Thus apple-trees, whose trunks are strong to bear
Their spreading boughs, exert themselves in air,
Want no supply, but stand secure alone,
Not trusting foreign forces, but their own,
Till with the ruddy freight the bending branches groan.

Thus trees of nature, and each common bush,
Uncultivated thrive, and with red berries blush.
Vile shrubs are shorn for browse; the towering height
Of unctuous trees are torches for the night.
And shall we doubt (indulging easy sloth),
To sow, to set, and to reform their growth?
To leave the lofty plants — the lowly kind
Are for the shepherd or the sheep designed.
E'en humble broom and osiers have their use,
And shade for sheep, and food for flocks, produce;
Hedges for corn, and honey for the bees,
Besides the pleasing prospect of the trees.
How goodly looks Cytorus, ever green
With boxen groves! with what delight are seen
Narycian woods of pitch, whose gloomy shade
Seems for retreat of heavenly muses made;
But much more pleasing are those fields to see,
That need not ploughs, nor human industry.

E'en cold Caucasean rocks with trees are spread,
And wear green forests on their hilly head.
Though bending from the blast of eastern storms,
Though shent their leaves, and scattered are their arms,
Yet heaven their various plants for use designs —
For houses, cedars — and, for shipping, pines —
Cypress provides for spokes and wheels of wains,
And all for keels of ships, that scour the watery plains.
Willows in twigs are fruitful, elms in leaves;
The war, from stubborn myrtle, shafts receives —
From cornels, javelins; and the tougher yew
Receives the bending figure of a bow.
Nor box, nor limes, without their use are made,
Smooth-grained, and proper for the turner's trade
Which curious hands may carve, and steel with ease invade.
Light alder stems the Po's impetuous tide,
And bees in hollow oaks their honey hide.
Now, balance with these gifts, the fumy joys
Of wine, attended with eternal noise,
Wine urged to lawless lust the Centaurs' train;
Through wine they quarreled, and through wine were slain.
   O happy, if he knew his happy state,
The swain, who, free from business and debate,
Receives his easy food from nature's hand,
And just returns of cultivated land!
No palace, with a lofty gate, he wants,
To admit the tides of early visitants,
With eager eyes devouring, as they pass,

The breathing figures of Corinthian brass.
No statues threaten, from high pedestals;
No Persian arras hides his homely walls,
With antic vests, which, through their shady fold,
Betray the streaks of ill-dissembled gold:
He boasts no wool, whose native white is dyed
With purple poison of Assyrian pride;
No costly drugs of Araby defile,
With foreign scents, the sweetness of his oil:
But easy quiet, a secure retreat,
A harmless life that knows not how to cheat,
With home-bred plenty, the rich owner bless,
And rural pleasures crown his happiness.
Unvexed with quarrels, undisturbed with noise,
The country king his peaceful realm enjoys —
Cool grots, and living lakes, the flowery pride
Of meads, and streams that through the valley glide,
And shady groves that easy sleep invite,
And after toilsome days, a soft repose at night.
Wild beasts of nature in his woods abound;
And youth, of labor patient, plough the ground,
Inured to hardship, and to homely fare.
Nor venerable age is wanting there,
In great examples to the youthful train;
Nor are the gods adored with rites profane.
From hence Astræa took her flight; and here
The prints of her departing steps appear.
  Ye sacred muses! with whose beauty fired,

My soul is ravished, and my brain inspired —
Whose priest I am, whose holy fillets wear —
Would you your poet's first petition hear;
Give me the ways of wandering stars to know,
The depths of heaven above, and earth below:
Teach me the various labors of the moon,
And whence proceed the eclipses of the sun;
Why flowing tides prevail upon the main,
And in what dark recess they shrink again;
What shakes the solid earth; what cause delays
The summer nights, and shortens winter days.
But, if my heavy blood restrain the flight
Of my free soul, aspiring to the height
Of nature, and unclouded fields of light —
My next desire is, void of care and strife,
To lead a soft, secure, inglorious life —
A country cottage near a crystal flood,
A winding valley, and a lofty wood.
Some god conduct me to the sacred shades,
Where Bacchanals are sung by Spartan maids,
Or lift me high to Hæmus' hilly crown,
Or in the plains of Tempè lay me down,
Or lead me to some solitary place,
And cover my retreat from human race.
　　Happy the man, who, studying nature's laws,
Through known effects can trace the secret cause —
His mind possessing in a quiet state,
Fearless of Fortune, and resigned to Fate!

And happy too is he, who decks the bowers
Of sylvans, and adores the rural powers —
Whose mind, unmoved, the bribes of courts can see,
Their glittering baits, and purple slavery —
Nor hopes the people's praise, nor fears their frown,
Nor, when contending kindred tear the crown,
Will set up one, or pull another down.
    Without concern he hears, but hears from far,
Of tumults, and descents, and distant war;
Nor with a superstitious fear is awed,
For what befalls at home, or what abroad.
Nor his own peace disturbs with pity for the poor.
Nor envies he the rich their happy store,
He feeds on fruits, which, of their own accord,
The willing ground and laden trees afford.
From his loved home no lucre him can draw;
The senate's mad decrees he never saw;
Nor heard, at bawling bars, corrupted law.
Some to the seas, and some to camps, resort,
And some with impudence invade the court;
In foreign countries, others seek renown;
With wars and taxes, others waste their own,
And houses burn, and household gods deface,
To drink in bowls which glittering gems enchase,
To loll on couches, rich with citron steds,
And lay their guilty limbs in Tyrian beds.
This wretch in earth entombs his golden ore,
Hovering and brooding on his buried store.

Some patriot fools to popular praise aspire
Of public speeches, which worse fools admire,
While, from both benches, with redoubled sounds,
The applause of lords and commoners abounds.
Some, through ambition, or through thirst of gold,
Have slain their brothers, or their country sold,
And, leaving their sweet homes, in exile run
To lands that lay beneath another sun.
   The peasant, innocent of all these ills,
With crooked ploughs the fertile fallows tills,
And the round year with daily labor fills.
And hence the country markets are supplied:
Enough remains for household charge beside,
His wife and tender children to sustain,
And gratefully to feed his dumb deserving train.
Nor cease his labors till the yellow field
A full return of bearded harvest yield —
A crop so plenteous, as the land to load,
O'ercome the crowded barns, and lodge on ricks abroad.
   Thus every several season is employed,
Some spent in toil, and some in ease enjoyed.
The yeaning ewes prevent the springing year;
The laden boughs their fruits in autumn bear:
'Tis then the vine her liquid harvest yields,
Baked in the sunshine of ascending fields.
The winter comes; and then the falling mast
For greedy swine provides a full repast:
Then olives, ground in mills, their fatness boast,

And winter fruits are mellowed by the frost.
His cares are eased with intervals of bliss;
His little children climbing for a kiss,
Welcome their father's late return at night;
His faithful bed is crowned with chaste delight.
His kine with swelling udders ready stand,
And, lowing for the pail, invite the milker's hand.
His wanton kids, with budding horns prepared,
Fight harmless battles in his homely yard:
Himself, in rustic pomp, on holidays,
To rural powers a just oblation pays,
And on the green his careless limbs displays.
The hearth is in the midst; the herdsmen, round
The cheerful fire, provoke his health in goblets crowned.
He calls on Bacchus, and propounds the prize;
The groom his fellow-groom at butts defies,
And bends his bow, and levels with his eyes;
Or, stript for wrestling, smears his limbs with oil,
And watches, with a trip his foe to foil.
  Such was the life the frugal Sabines led;
So Remus and his brother-god were bred,
From whom the austere Etrurian virtue rose;
And this rude life our homely fathers chose.
Old Rome from such a race derived her birth
(The seat of empire and the conquered earth),
Which now on seven high hills triumphant reigns,
And in that compass all the world contains.
Ere Saturn's rebel son usurped the skies,

When beasts were only slain for sacrifice,
While peaceful Crete enjoyed her ancient lord,
Ere sounding hammers forged the inhuman sword,
Ere hollow drums were beat, before the breath
Of brazen trumpets rung the peals of death,
The good old god his hunger did assuage
With roots and herbs, and gave the golden age.
    But, over-labored with so long a course,
'Tis time to set at ease the smoking horse.

THE THIRD GEORGIC

THE ARGUMENT

This book begins with the invocation of some rural deities, and a compliment to Augustus; after which Virgil directs himself to Maecenas, and enters on his subject. He lays down rules for the breeding and management of horses, oxen, sheep, goats, and dogs; and interweaves several pleasant descriptions of a chariot-race, of the battle of the bulls, of the force of love, and of the Scythian winter. In the latter part of the book, he relates the diseases incident to cattle; and ends with the description of a fatal murrain that formerly raged among the Alps.

Thy fields, propitious Pales, I rehearse;
And sing thy pastures in no vulgar verse,
Amphrysian shepherd! the Lycæan woods,
Arcadia's flowery plains, and pleasing floods.
   All other themes, that careless minds invite,
Are worn with use, unworthy me to write.
Busiris' altars, and the dire decrees
Of hard Eurystheus, every reader sees:
Hylas the boy, Latona's erring isle,
And Pelops' ivory shoulder, and his toil
For fair Hippodamè, with all the rest
Of Grecian tales, by poets are expressed.
New ways I must attempt, my grovelling name
To raise aloft, and wing my flight to fame.
   I, first of Romans, shall in triumph come
From conquered Greece, and bring her trophies home,
With foreign spoils adorn my native place,
And with Idume's palms my Mantua grace.

Of Parian stone a temple will I raise,
Where the slow Mincius through the valley strays,
Where cooling streams invite the flocks to drink,
And reeds defend the winding water's brink.
Full in the midst shall mighty Cæsar stand,
Hold the chief honors, and the dome command.
Then I, conspicuous in my Tyrian gown
(Submitting to his godhead my renown),
A hundred coursers from the goal will drive:
The rival chariots in the race shall strive.
All Greece shall flock from far, my games to see;
The whorlbat, and the rapid race, shall be
Reserved for Cæsar, and ordained by me.
Myself, with olive crowned, the gifts will bear.
E'en now methinks the public shouts I hear;
The passing pageants, and the pomps appear.
I to the temple will conduct the crew,
The sacrifice and sacrificers view,
From thence return, attended with my train,
Where the proud theatres disclose the scene,
Which interwoven Britons seem to raise,
And show the triumph which their shame displays.
High o'er the gate, in elephant and gold,
The crowd shall Cæsar's Indian war behold:
The Nile shall flow beneath; and on the side
His shattered ships on brazen pillars ride.
Next him Niphates, with inverted urn,
And drooping sedge, shall his Armenian mourn;

And Asian cities in our triumph borne.
With backward bows the Parthians shall be there,
And, spurring from the fight, confess their fear.
A double wreath shall crown our Cæsar's brows —
Two differing trophies, from two different foes.
Europe with Afric in his fame shall join;
But neither shore his conquest shall confine.
The Parian marble there shall seem to move
In breathing statues, not unworthy Jove,
Resembling heroes, whose ethereal root
Is Jove himself, and Cæsar is the fruit.
Tros and his race the sculptor shall employ;
And he — the god who built the walls of Troy.
Envy herself at last, grown pale and dumb
(By Cæsar combated and overcome),
Shall give her hands, and fear the curling snakes
Of lashing Furies, and the burning lakes;
The pains of famished Tantalus shall feel,
And Sisyphus, that labors up the hill
The rolling rock in vain; and curts Ixion's wheel.
   Meantime we must pursue the sylvan lands
(The abode of nymphs), untouched by former hands;
For such, Mæcenas, are thy hard commands.
Without thee, nothing lofty can I sing:
Come then, and, with thyself, thy genius bring,
With which inspired, I brook no dull delay:
Cithæron loudly calls me to my way;
Thy hounds, Taygetus, open, and pursue their prey.

High Epidaurus urges on my speed,
Famed for his hills, and for his horses' breed:
From hills and dales the cheerful cries rebound;
For Echo hunts along, and propagates the sound.

A time will come, when my maturer muse,
In Cæsar's wars, a nobler theme shall choose,
And through more ages bear my sovereign's praise,
Than have from Tithon past to Cæsar's days.

The generous youth, who, studious of the prize,
The race of running coursers multiplies,
Or to the plough the sturdy bullock breeds,
May know, that from the dam the worth of each proceeds.
The mother-cow must wear a lowering look,
Sour-headed, strongly necked, to bear the yoke.
Her double dewlap from her chin descends,
And at her thighs the ponderous burden ends.
Long are her sides and large; her limbs are great;
Rough are her ears, and broad her horny feet.
Her color shining black, but flecked with white;
She tosses from the yoke; provokes the fight:
She rises in her gait, is free from fears,
And in her face a bull's resemblance bears:
Her ample forehead with a star is crowned,
And with her length of tail she sweeps the ground,
The bull's insult at four she may sustain;
But, after ten, from nuptial rites refrain.
Six seasons use; but then release the cow,
Unfit for love, and for the laboring plough.

Now, while their youth is filled with kindly fire
Submit thy females to the lusty sire:
Watch the quick motions of the frisking tail;
Then serve their fury with the rushing male,
Indulging pleasure, lest the breed should fail.

In youth alone unhappy mortals live;
But ah! the mighty bliss is fugitive:
Discolored sickness, anxious labors, come,
And age, and death's inexorable doom.

Yearly thy herds in vigor will impair.
Recruit and mend them with thy yearly care:
Still propagate; for still they fall away:
'Tis prudence to prevent the entire decay.

Like diligence requires the courser's race,
In early choice, and for a longer space,
The colt, that for a stallion is designed,
By sure presages shows his generous kind:
Of able body, sound of limb and wind,
Upright he walks, on pasterns firm and straight;
His motions easy; prancing in his gait;
The first to lead the way, to tempt the flood,
To pass the bridge unknown, nor fear the trembling
    wood;
Dauntless at empty noises; lofty necked;
Sharp-headed, barrel-bellied, broadly-backed:
Brawny his chest, and deep; his color gray;
For beauty, dappled, or the brightest bay:
Faint white and dun will scarce the rearing pay.

The fiery courser, when he hears from far
The sprightly trumpets, and the shouts of war,
Pricks up his ears; and, trembling with delight,
Shifts place, and paws, and hopes the promised fight.
On his right shoulder his thick mane reclined,
Ruffles at speed, and dances in the wind.
His horny hoofs are jetted black and round;
His chine is double; starting with a bound
He turns the turf, and shakes the solid ground.
Fire from his eyes, clouds from his nostrils, flow:
He bears his rider headlong on the foe.
  Such was the steed in Grecian poets famed,
Proud Cyllarus, by Spartan Pollux tamed:
Such coursers bore to fight the god of Thrace:
And such, Achilles, was thy warlike race,
In such a shape, grim Saturn did restrain
His heavenly limbs, and flowed with such a mane,
When, half-surprised, and fearing to be seen,
The lecher galloped from his jealous queen;
Ran up the ridges of the rocks amain,
And with shrill neighings filled the neighboring plain.
  But, worn with years, when dire diseases come,
Then hide his not ignoble age at home,
In peace to enjoy his former palms and pains;
And gratefully be kind to his remains.
For, when his blood no youthful spirits move,
He languishes and labors in his love;
And, when the sprightly seed should swiftly come,

Dribbling he drudges, and defrauds the womb.
In vain he burns, like hasty stubble fires,
And in himself his former self requires.
  His age and courage weigh; nor those alone,
But note his father's virtues and his own;
Observe if he disdains to yield the prize,
Of loss impatient, proud of victories.
  Hast thou beheld, when from the goal they start,
The youthful charioteers with heaving heart
Rush to the race; and, panting, scarcely bear
The extremes of feverish hope and chilling fear;
Stoop to the reins, and lash with all their force?
The flying chariot kindles in the course:
And now alow, and now aloft, they fly,
As borne through air, and seem to touch the sky.
No stop, no stay: but clouds of sand arise,
Spurned and cast backward on the followers' eyes
The hindmost blows the foam upon the first;
Such is the love of praise, an honorable thirst.
  Bold Erichthonius was the first who joined
Four horses for the rapid race designed,
And o'er the dusty wheels presiding sat:
The Lapithæ, to chariots, add the state
Of bits and bridles; taught the steed to bound,
To run the ring, and trace the mazy round;
To stop, to fly, the rules of war to know;
To obey the rider, and to dare the foe.
  To choose a youthful steed with courage fired,

To breed him, break him, back him, are required
Experienced masters; and, in sundry ways,
Their labors equal, and alike their praise.
But, once again, the battered horse beware:
The weak old stallion will deceive thy care,

Though famous in his youth for force and speed,
Or was of Argos or Epirian breed,
Or did from Neptune's race, or from himself, proceed.
　These things premised, when now the nuptial time
Approaches for the stately steed to climb,
With food enable him to make his court;
Distend his chine, and pamper him for sport:
Feed him with herbs, whatever thou canst find,
Of generous warmth, and of salacious kind:
Then water him, and (drinking what he can)
Encourage him to thirst again, with bran.
Instructed thus, produce him to the fair,
And join in wedlock to the longing mare.

For, if the sire be faint, or out of case,
He will be copied in his famished race,
And sink beneath the pleasing task assigned
(For all's too little for the craving kind).
   As for the females, with industrious care
Take down their mettle; keep them lean and bare:
When conscious of their past delight, and keen
To take the leap, and prove the sport again,
With scanty measure then supply their food;
And, when athirst, restrain them from the flood;
Their bodies harass; sink them when they run;
And fry their melting marrow in the sun.
Starve them, when barns beneath their burden groan,
And winnowed chaff by western winds is blown;
For fear the rankness of the swelling womb
Should scant the passage, and confine the room;
Lest the fat furrows should the sense destroy
Of genial lust, and dull the seat of joy.
But let them suck the seed with greedy force,
And close involve the vigor of the horse.
The male has done: thy care must now proceed
To teeming females, and the promised breed.
First let them run at large, and never know
The taming yoke, or draw the crooked plough.
Let them not leap the ditch, or swim the flood,
Or lumber o'er the meads, or cross the wood;
But range the forest, by the silver side
Of some cool stream, where nature shall provide

Green grass and fattening clover for their fare,
And mossy caverns for their noontide lair,
With rocks above, to shield the sharp nocturnal air.
  About the Alburnian groves, with holly green,
Of wingèd insects mighty swarms are seen:
This flying plague (to mark its quality)
Œstros the Grecians call — Asylus, we —
A fierce loud-buzzing breeze — their stings draw blood,
And drive the cattle gadding through the wood.
Seized with unusual pains, they loudly cry:
Tanagrus hastens thence, and leaves his channel dry.
This curse the jealous Juno did invent,
And first employed for Iö's punishment.
To shun this ill, the cunning leech ordains,
In summer's sultry heats (for then it reigns)
To feed the females ere the sun arise,
Or late at night, when stars adorn the skies.
When she has calved, then set the dam aside,
And for the tender progeny provide.
Distinguish all betimes with branding fire,
To note the tribe, the lineage and the sire;
Whom to reserve for husband of the herd;
Or who shall be to sacrifice preferred;
Or whom thou shalt to turn thy glebe allow,
To smooth the furrows, and sustain the plough:
The rest, for whom no lot is yet decreed,
May run in pastures, and at pleasure feed.
  The calf, by nature and by genius made

To turn the glebe, breed to the rural trade.
Set him betimes to school: and let him be
Instructed there in rules of husbandry,
While yet his youth is flexible and green,
Nor bad examples of the world has seen.
Early begin the stubborn child to break:
For his soft neck, a supple collar make
Of bending osiers; and (with time and care
Inured that easy servitude to bear)
Thy flattering method on the youth pursue:
Joined with his schoolfellows by two and two,
Persuade them first to lead an empty wheel,
That scarce the dust can raise, or they can feel:
In length of time produce the laboring yoke,
And shining shares, that make the furrow smoke.
Ere the licentious youth be thus restrained,
Or moral precepts on their minds have gained,
Their wanton appetites not only feed
With delicates of leaves, and marshy weed,
But with thy sickle reap the rankest land,
And minister the blade with bounteous hand:
Nor be with harmful parsimony won
To follow what our homely sires have done,
Who filled the pail with beestings of the cow,
But all her udder to the calf allow.
    If to the warlike steed thy studies bend,
Or for the prize in chariots to contend,
Near Pisa's flood the rapid wheels to guide,

Or in Olympian groves aloft to ride,
The generous labors of the courser, first,
Must be with sight of arms and sounds of trumpets
   nursed;
Inured the groaning axle-tree to bear,
And let him clashing whips in stables hear.
Sooth him with praise, and make him understand
The loud applauses of his master's hand:
This, from his weaning, let him well be taught:
And then betimes in a soft snaffle wrought,
Before his tender joints with nerves are knit,
Untried in arms, and trembling at the bit.
But, when to four full springs his years advance,
Teach him to run the ground, with pride to prance,
And (rightly managed) equal time to beat,
To turn, to bound in measure, and curvet.
Let him to this, with easy pains, be brought,
And seem to labor, when he labors not.
Thus formed for speed, he challenges the wind,
And leaves the Scythian arrow far behind:
He scours along the field, with loosened reins,
And treads so light, he scarcely prints the plains;
Like Boreas in his race, when, rushing forth,
He sweeps the skies, and clears the cloudy north:
The waving harvest bends beneath his blast,
The forest shakes, the groves their honors cast;
He flies aloft, and with impetuous roar
Pursues the foaming surges to the shore.

Thus, o'er the Elean plains, thy well-breathed horse
Impels the flying car, and wins the course,
Or, bred to Belgian waggons, leads the way,
Untired at night, and cheerful all the day.
   When once he's broken, feed him full and high;
Indulge his growth, and his gaunt sides supply.
Before his training, keep him poor and low;
For his stout stomach with his food will grow;
The pampered colt will discipline disdain,
Impatient of the lash, and restive to the rein.
Wouldst thou their courage and their strength improve?
Too soon they must not feel the stings of love.
Whether the bull or courser be thy care,
Let him not leap the cow, or mount the mare.
The youthful bull must wander in the wood,
Behind the mountain, or beyond the flood,
Or in the stall at home his fodder find,
Far from the charms of that alluring kind.
With two fair eyes his mistress burns his breast:
He looks, and languishes, and leaves his rest,
Forsakes his food, and, pining for the lass,
Is joyless of the grove, and spurns the growing grass.
The soft seducer, with enticing looks,
The bellowing rivals to the fight provokes.
   A beauteous heifer in the wood is bred:
The stooping warriors, aiming head to head,
Engage their clashing horns: with dreadful sound
The forest rattles, and the rocks rebound.

They fence, they push, and, pushing, loudly roar:
Their dewlaps and their sides are bathed in gore.
Nor, when the war is over, is it peace;
Nor will the vanquished bull his claim release;
But, feeding in his breast his ancient fires,
And cursing fate, from his proud foe retires.
Driven from his native land to foreign grounds,
He with a generous rage resents his wounds,
His ignominious flight, the victor's boast,
And, more than both, the loves which unrevenged
   he lost.
Often he turns his eyes, and, with a groan,
Surveys the pleasing kingdoms, once his own:
And therefore to repair his strength he tries,
Hardening his limbs with painful exercise,
And rough upon the flinty rock he lies.
On prickly leaves and on sharp herbs he feeds,
Then to the prelude of a war proceeds.
His horns, yet sore, he tries against a tree,
And meditates his absent enemy.
He snuffs the wind; his heels the sand excite;
But, when he stands collected in his might,
He roars, and promises a more successful fight.
Then, to redeem his honor at a blow,
He moves his camp, to meet his careless foe.
Not with more madness, rolling from afar,
The spumy waves proclaim the watery war,
And mounting upwards, with a mighty roar,

March onwards, and insult the rocky shore.
They mate the middle region with their height,
And fall no less than with a mountain's weight;
The waters boil, and, belching, from below
Black sands, as from a forceful engine, throw.
   Thus every creature, and of every kind,
The secret joys of sweet coition find.
Not only man's imperial race, but they
That wing the liquid air, or swim the sea,
Or haunt the desert, rush into the flame:
For Love is lord of all, and is in all the same.
   'Tis with this rage, the mother-lion stung,
Scours o'er the plain, regardless of her young:
Demanding rites of love, she sternly stalks,
And hunts her lover in his lonely walks.
'Tis then the shapeless bear his den forsakes;
In woods and fields, a wild destruction makes:
Boars with their tusks; to battle tigers move,
Enraged with hunger, more enraged with love.
Then woe to him, that, in the desert land
Of Libya, travels o'er the burning sand!
The stallion snuffs the well-known scent afar,
And snorts and trembles for the distant mare;
Nor bits nor bridles can his rage restrain,
And rugged rocks are interposed in vain:
He makes his way o'er mountains, and contemns
Unruly torrents, and unforded streams.
The bristled boar, who feels the pleasing wound,

New grinds his arming tusks, and digs the ground.
The sleepy lecher shuts his little eyes;
About his churning chaps the frothy bubbles rise;
He rubs his sides against a tree; prepares
And hardens both his shoulders for the wars.

What did the youth, when Love's unerring dart
Transfixed his liver, and inflamed his heart?
Alone, by night, his watery way he took;
About him, and above, the billows broke;
The sluices of the sky were open spread,
And rolling thunder rattled o'er his head;
The raging tempests called him back in vain,
And every boding omen of the main:
Nor could his kindred, nor the kindly force
Of weeping parents, change his fatal course;
No, not the dying maid, who must deplore
His floating carcase on the Sestian shore.

I pass the wars that spotted lynxes make
With their fierce rivals for the female's sake,
The howling wolves', the mastiffs' amorous rage;
When e'en the fearful stag dares for his kind engage.
But, far above the rest, the furious mare,
Barred from the male, is frantic with despair:
For when her pouting vent declares her pain,
She tears the harness, and she rends the rein.
For this (when Venus gave them rage and power)
Their master's mangled members they devour,
Of love defrauded in their longing hour.

For love, they force through thickets of the wood,
They climb the steepy hills, and stem the flood.
  When, at the spring's approach, their marrow burns
(For with the spring their genial warmth returns),
The mares to cliffs of rugged rocks repair,
And with wide nostrils snuff the western air:
When (wondrous to relate!) the parent wind,
Without the stallion, propagates the kind,
Then, fired with amorous rage, they take their flight
Through plains, and mount the hills' unequal height;
Nor to the north, nor to the rising sun,
Nor southward to the rainy regions, run,
But boring to the west, and hovering there,
With gaping mouths, they draw prolific air;
With which impregnate, from their groins they shed,
A slimy juice, by false conception bred.
The shepherd knows it well, and calls by name
Hippomanes, to note the mother's flame.
This, gathered in the planetary hour,
With noxious weeds, and spelled with words of power,
Dire stepdames in the magic bowl infuse,
And mix, for deadly draughts, the poisonous juice.
  But time is lost, which never will renew,
While we too far the pleasing path pursue,
Surveying nature with too nice a view.
Let this suffice for herds; our following care
Shall woolly flocks and shaggy goats declare.
Nor can I doubt what toil I must bestow,

To raise my subject from a ground so low;
And the mean matter, which my theme affords,
To embellish with magnificence of words.
But the commanding muse my chariot guides,
Which o'er the dubious cliff securely rides;
And pleased I am, no beaten road to take,
But first the way to new discoveries make.
   Now, sacred Pales! in a lofty strain
I sing the rural honors of thy reign.
First, with assiduous care from winter keep,
Well foddered in the stalls, thy tender sheep:
Then spread with straw the bedding of thy fold,
With fern beneath, to 'fend the bitter cold;
That free from gouts thou mayest preserve thy care,
And clear from scabs, produced by freezing air.
Next let thy goats officiously be nursed,
And led to living streams, to quench their thirst.
Feed them with winter-browse; and, for their lair,
A cote, that opens to the south, prepare;
Where basking in the sunshine they may lie,
And the short remnants of his heat enjoy.
This during winter's drizzly reign be done,
Till the new Ram receives the exalted sun.
For hairy goats of equal profit are
With woolly sheep, and ask an equal care.
'Tis true, the fleece, when drunk with Tyrian juice,
Is dearly sold; but not for needful use;
For the salacious goat increases more,

And twice as largely yields her milky store.
The still-distended udders never fail,
But, when they seem exhausted, swell the pail.
Meantime the pastor shears their hoary beards,
And eases of their hair the laden herds.
Their camelots, warm in tents, the soldier hold,
And shield the shivering mariner from cold.
   On shrubs they browse, and, on the bleaky top
Of rugged hills, the thorny bramble crop.
Attended with their bleating kids, they come
At night, unasked, and mindful of their home;
And scarce their swelling bags the threshold overcome.
So much the more thy diligence bestow
In depth of winter, to defend the snow,
By how much less the tender helpless kind,
For their own ills, can fit provision find.
Then minister the browse with bounteous hand,
And open let thy sacks all winter stand.
But, when the western winds with vital power
Call forth the tender grass and budding flower,
Then, at the last, produce, in open air
Both flocks, and send them to their summer fare.
Before the sun while Hesperus appears,
First let them sip from herbs the pearly tears
Of morning dews, and after break their fast
On greensward ground — a cool and grateful taste.
But, when the day's fourth hour has drawn the dews,
And the sun's sultry heat their thirst renews;

When creaking grasshoppers on shrubs complain,
Then lead them to their watering-troughs again.
In summer's heat, some bending valley find,
Closed from the sun, but open to the wind;
Or seek some ancient oak, whose arms extend
In ample breadth, thy cattle to defend,
Or solitary grove, or gloomy glade,
To shield them with its venerable shade.
Once more to watering lead; and feed again
When the low sun is sinking to the main,
When rising Cynthia sheds her silver dews,
And the cool evening-breeze the meads renews,
When linnets fill the wood with tuneful sound,
And hollow shores the halcyon's voice rebound.

Why should my muse enlarge on Libyan swains,
Their scattered cottages, and ample plains,
Where oft the flocks without a leader stray,
Or through continued desert take their way,
And, feeding, add the length of night to day?
Whole months they wander, grazing as they go;
Nor folds nor hospitable harbor know:
Such an extent of plains, so vast a space
Of wilds unknown, and of untasted grass,
Allures their eyes: the shepherd last appears,
And with him all his patrimony bears,
His house, and household gods, his trade of war,
His bow and quiver, and his trusty cur.
Thus, under heavy arms, the youth of Rome

Their long laborious marches overcome,
Cheerly their tedious travels undergo,
And pitch their sudden camp before the foe.
  Not so the Scythian shepherd tends his fold,
Nor he who bears in Thrace the bitter cold,
Nor he who treads the bleak Mæotian strand,
Or where proud Ister rolls his yellow sand.
Early they stall their flocks and herds; for there
No grass the fields, no leaves the forests, wear:
The frozen earth lies buried there, below
A hilly heap, seven cubits deep in snow;
And all the west allies of stormy Boreas blow.
  The sun from far peeps with a sickly face,
Too weak, the clouds and mighty fogs to chase,
When up the skies he shoots his rosy head,
Or in the ruddy ocean seeks his bed.
Swift rivers are with sudden ice constrained;
And studded wheels are on its back sustained;
A hostry now for waggons, which before
Tall ships of burden on its bosom bore.
The brazen caldrons with the frost are flawed;
The garment, stiff with ice, at hearths is thawed;
With axes first they cleave the wine; and thence,
By weight, the solid portions they dispense.
From locks uncombed, and from the frozen beard,
Long icicles depend, and crackling sounds are heard.
Meantime perpetual sleet and driving snow,
Obscure the skies, and hang on herds below.

The starving cattle perish in their stalls;
Huge oxen stand inclosed in wintry walls
Of snow congealed; whole herds are buried there
Of mighty stags, and scarce their horns appear.
The dexterous huntsman wounds not these afar
With shafts or darts, or makes a distant war
With dogs, or pitches toils to stop their flight,
But close engages in unequal fight;
And, while they strive in vain to make their way
Through hills of snow, and pitifully bray,
Assaults with dint of sword, or pointed spears,
And homeward, on his back, the joyful burden bears.
The men to subterranean caves retire,
Secure from cold, and crowd the cheerful fire;
With trunks of elms and oaks the hearth they load,
Nor tempt the clemency of heaven abroad.
Their jovial nights in frolics and in play
They pass, to drive the tedious hours away,
And their cold stomachs with crowned goblets cheer
Of windy cider, and of barmy beer.
Such are the cold Rhipæan race, and such
The savage Scythian, and unwarlike Dutch,
Where skins of beasts the rude barbarians wear,
The spoils of foxes, and the furry bear.

   Is wool thy care? let not thy cattle go
Where bushes are, where burs and thistles grow;
Nor in too rank a pasture let them feed;
Then of the purest white select thy breed.

E'en though a snowy ram thou shalt behold,
Prefer him not in haste for husband to thy fold:
But search his mouth; and if a swarthy tongue
Is underneath his humid palate hung,
Reject him, lest he darken all the flock,
And substitute another from thy stock.
'Twas thus, with fleeces milky-white (if we
May trust report), Pan, god of Arcady,
Did bribe thee, Cynthia; nor didst thou disdain,
When called in woody shades, to cure a lover's pain.

  If milk be thy design, with plenteous hand
Bring clover-grass; and from the marshy land
Salt herbage for the foddering rack provide,
To fill their bags, and swell the milky tide.
These raise their thirst, and to the taste restore
The savor of the salt, on which they fed before.

  Some, when the kids their dams too deeply drain,
With gags and muzzles their soft mouths restrain.
Their morning milk the peasants press at night;
Their evening meal, before the rising light,
To market bear; or sparingly they steep
With seasoning salt, and stored for winter keep.

  Nor, last, forget thy faithful dogs; but feed
With fattening whey the mastiff's generous breed,
And Spartan race, who, for the fold's relief,
Will persecute with cries the nightly thief,
Repulse the prowling wolf, and hold at bay
The mountain robbers rushing to the prey.

With cries of hounds, thou may'st pursue the fear
Of flying hares, and chase the fallow deer,
Rouse from their desert dens the bristled rage
Of boars, and beamy stags in toils engage.

With smoke of burning cedar scent thy walls,
And fume with stinking galbanum thy stalls,
With that rank odor, from thy dwelling-place
To drive the viper's brood, and all the venomed race:
For often, under stalls unmoved, they lie,
Obscure in shades, and shunning heaven's broad eye:
And snakes, familiar, to the hearth succeed,
Disclose their eggs, and near the chimney breed —
Whether to roofy houses they repair,
Or sun themselves abroad in open air,
In all abodes, of pestilential kind
To sheep and oxen, and the painful hind.
Take, shepherd, take a plant of stubborn oak,
And labor him with many a sturdy stroke,

Or with hard stones demolish from afar
His haughty crest, the seat of all the war;
Invade his hissing throat, and winding spires;
Till, stretched in length, the unfolded foe retires.
He drags his tail, and for his head provides,
And in some secret cranny slowly glides;
But leaves exposed to blows his back and battered sides.
   In fair Calabria's woods a snake is bred,
With curling crest, and with advancing head:
Waving he rolls, and makes a winding track;
His belly spotted, burnished is his back.
While springs are broken, while the southern air
And dropping heavens the moistened earth repair,
He lives on standing lakes and trembling bogs,
And fills his maw with fish, or with loquacious frogs:
But when, in muddy pools, the water sinks,
And the chapped earth is furrowed o'er with chinks,
He leaves the fens, and leaps upon the ground,
And, hissing, rolls his glaring eyes around.
With thirst inflamed, impatient of the heats,
He rages in the fields, and wide destruction threats.
O! let not sleep my closing eyes invade
In open plains, or in the secret shade,
When he, renewed in all the speckled pride
Of pompous youth, has cast his slough aside,
And in his summer livery rolls along,
Erect, and brandishing his forky tongue,
Leaving his nest, and his imperfect young,

And, thoughtless of his eggs, forgets to rear
The hopes of poison for the following year.
   The causes and the signs shall next be told,
Of every sickness that infects the fold.
A scabby tetter on their pelts will stick,
When the raw rain has pierced them to the quick,
Or searching frosts have eaten through the skin,
Or burning icicles are lodged within;
Or, when the fleece is shorn, if sweat remains
Unwashed, and soaks into their empty veins;
When their defenceless limbs the brambles tear,
Short of their wool, and naked from the shear.
   Good shepherds, after shearing, drench their sheep!
And their flock's father (forced from high to leap)
Swims down the stream, and plunges in the deep.
They oint their naked limbs with mothered oil;
Or, from the founts where living sulphurs boil,
They mix a med'cine to foment their limbs,
With scum that on the molten silver swims:
Fat pitch, and black bitumen, add to these,
Besides the waxen labor of the bees,
And hellebore, and squills deep-rooted in the seas.
Receipts abound; but, searching all thy store,
The best is still at hand, to lance the sore,
And cut the head; for, till the core be found,
The secret vice is fed, and gathers ground,
While, making fruitless moan, the shepherd stands,
And, when the lancing-knife requires his hands,

Vain help, with idle prayers, from heaven demands.
Deep in their bones when fevers fix their seat,
And rack their limbs, and lick the vital heat,
The ready cure to cool the raging pain
Is underneath the foot to breathe a vein.
This remedy the Scythian shepherds found:
The inhabitants of Thracia's hilly ground,
And Gelons, use it, when for drink and food
They mix their curdled milk with horses' blood.
But, where thou seest a single sheep remain
In shades aloof, or couched upon the plain,
Or listlessly to crop the tender grass,
Or late to lag behind with truant pace;
Revenge the crime, and take the traitor's head,
Ere in the faultless flock the dire contagion spread.

   On winter seas we fewer storms behold,
Than foul diseases that infect the fold.
Nor do those ills on single bodies prey,
But oftener bring the nation to decay,
And sweep the present stock and future hope away.
   A dire example of this truth appears,
When, after such a length of rolling years,
We see the naked Alps, and thin remains
Of scattered cots, and yet unpeopled plains,
Once filled with grazing flocks, the shepherds' happy reigns.
   Here, from the vicious air, and sickly skies,
A plague did on the dumb creation rise:
During the autumnal heats the infection grew,

Tame cattle and the beasts of nature slew,
Poisoning the standing lakes, and pools impure;
Nor was the foodful grass in fields secure.
Strange death! for, when the thirsty fire had drunk
Their vital blood, and the dry nerves were shrunk,
When the contracted limbs were cramped, e'en then
A waterish humor swelled and oozed again,
Converting into bane the kindly juice,
Ordained by nature for a better use.
   The victim ox, that was for altars prest,
Trimmed with white ribbons, and with garlands drest,
Sunk of himself, without the gods' command,
Preventing the slow sacrificer's hand.
Or, by the holy butcher if he fell,
The inspected entrails could no fates foretell;
Nor, laid on altars, did pure flames arise;
But clouds of smouldering smoke forbade the sacrifice.
Scarcely the knife was reddened with his gore,
Or the black poison stained the sandy floor.
The thriven calves in meads their food forsake,
And render their sweet souls before the plenteous rack.
   The fawning dog runs mad; the wheezing swine
With coughs is choked, and labors from the chine:
The victor horse, forgetful of his food,
The palm renounces, and abhors the flood.
He paws the ground; and on his hanging ears
A doubtful sweat in clammy drops appears:
Parched is his hide, and rugged are his hairs.

Such are the symptoms of the young disease;
But, in time's process, when his pains increase,
He rolls his mournful eyes; he deeply groans
With patient sobbing, and with manly moans.
He heaves for breath; which, from his lungs supplied,
And fetched from far, distends his laboring side.
To his rough palate his dry tongue succeeds;
And ropy gore he from his nostrils bleeds.
A drench of wine has with success been used,
And through a horn the generous juice infused,
Which, timely taken, oped his closing jaws,
But, if too late, the patient's death did cause:
For the too vigorous dose too fiercely wrought,
And added fury to the strength it brought.
Recruited into rage, he grinds his teeth
In his own flesh, and feeds approaching death.
Ye gods, to better fate good men dispose,
And turn that impious error on our foes!
　　The steer, who to the yoke was bred to bow
(Studious of tillage, and the crooked plough),
Falls down and dies; and, dying, spews a flood
Of foamy madness, mixed with clotted blood.
The clown, who, cursing Providence, repines,
His mournful fellow from the team disjoins;
With many a groan forsakes his fruitless care,
And in the unfinished furrow leaves the share.
The pining steer nor shades of lofty woods,
Nor flowery meads can ease, nor crystal floods

Rolled from the rock: his flabby flanks decrease;
His eyes are settled in a stupid peace;
His bulk too weighty for his thighs is grown,
And his unwieldy neck hangs drooping down.
Now what avails his well-deserving toil
To turn the glebe, or smooth the rugged soil?
And yet he never supped in solemn state
(Nor undigested feasts did urge his fate),
Nor day to night luxuriously did join,
Nor surfeited on rich Campanian wine.
Simple his beverage, homely was his food,
The wholesome herbage, and the running flood:
No dreadful dreams awaked him with affright;
His pains by day, secured his rest by night.
  'Twas then that buffaloes, ill paired, were seen
To draw the car of Jove's imperial queen,
For want of oxen; and the laboring swain
Scratched with a rake, a furrow for his grain,
And covered with his hand the shallow seed again.
He yokes himself, and up the hilly height,
With his own shoulders, draws the waggon's weight.
  The nightly wolf, that round the inclosure prowled,
To leap the fence, now plots not on the fold,
Tamed with a sharper pain. The fearful doe,
And flying stag, amidst the greyhounds go,
And round the dwellings roam of man, their fiercer foe.
The scaly nations of the sea profound,
Like shipwrecked carcasses, are driven aground,

And mighty phocæ, never seen before
In shallow streams, are stranded on the shore.
The viper dead within her hole is found:
Defenceless was the shelter of the ground.
The water-snake, whom fish and paddocks fed,
With staring scales lies poisoned in his bed:
To birds their native heavens contagious prove;
From clouds they fall, and leave their souls above.

    Besides, to change their pasture 'tis in vain,
Or trust to physic; physic is their bane.
The learnèd leeches in despair depart,
And shake their heads, desponding of their art.

    Tisiphone, let loose from under ground,
Majestically pale, now treads the round,
Before her drives diseases and affright,
And every moment rises to the sight,
Aspiring to the skies, encroaching on the light.
The rivers, and their banks, and hills around,
With lowings and with dying bleats resound.
At length, she strikes a universal blow;
To death at once whole herds of cattle go;
Sheep, oxen, horses, fall; and heaped on high,
The differing species in confusion lie,
Till, warned by frequent ills, the way they found
To lodge their loathsome carrion under ground:
For useless to the currier were their hides;
Nor could their tainted flesh with ocean tides
Be freed from filth; nor could Vulcanian flame

107

The stench abolish, or the savor tame.
Nor safely could they shear their fleecy store
(Made drunk with poisonous juice, & stiff with gore),
Or touch the web: but, if the vest they wear,
Red blisters rising on their paps appear,
And flaming carbuncles, and noisome sweat,
And clammy dews, that loathsome lice beget;
Till the slow-creeping evil eats his way,
Consumes the parching limbs, & makes the life his prey.

THE FOURTH GEORGIC

THE ARGUMENT

Virgil has taken care to raise the subject of each Georgic. In the first, he deals only with dead matter. In the second, he just steps on the world of life, and describes that of vegetables. In the third, he advances to animals: and in the last, he singles out the bee, the most sagacious of them, for his subject. In this Georgic, he shews us what station is most proper for the bees, and when they begin to gather honey; how to call them home when they swarm, and how to part them when they are engaged in battle. From hence he takes occasion to discover their different kinds; and, after an excursion, relates their prudent and politic administration of affairs, and the diseases that often rage in their hives, with the proper symptoms and remedies of each. In the last place he lays down a method of repairing their kind, supposing their whole breed lost; and gives the history of its invention.

The gifts of Heaven my following song pursues
Aërial honey, and ambrosial dews.
Mæcenas, read this other part, that sings
Embattled squadrons and adventurous kings —
A mighty pomp, though made of little things.
Their arms, their arts, their manners, I disclose,
And how they war, and whence the people rose.
Slight is the subject, but the praise not small,
If Heaven assist, and Phœbus hear my call.
    First, for thy bees a quiet station find,
And lodge them under covert of the wind
(For winds, when homeward they return, will drive
The loaded carriers from their evening hive),
Far from the cows' and goats' insulting crew,
That trample down the flowers, and brush the dew.
The painted lizard, and the birds of prey,
Foes of the frugal kind, be far away —
The titmouse, and the pecker's hungry brood,

And Procne, with her bosom stained in blood:
These rob the trading citizens, and bear
The trembling captives through the liquid air,
And for their callow young a cruel feast prepare.
But near a living stream their mansion place,
Edged round with moss, and tufts of matted grass:
And plant (the winds' impetuous rage to stop)
Wild olive trees, or palms, before the busy shop;
That, when the youthful prince, with proud alarm,
Calls out the venturous colony to swarm —
When first their way through yielding air they wing,
New to the pleasures of their native spring —
The banks of brooks may make a cool retreat
For the raw soldiers from the scalding heat,
And neighboring trees with friendly shade invite
The troops, unused to long laborious flight.
Then o'er the running stream, or standing lake,
A passage for thy weary people make;
With osier floats the standing water strew;
Of massy stones make bridges, if it flow;
That basking in the sun thy bees may lie,
And resting there, their flaggy pinions dry,
When late returning home, the laden host
By raging winds is wrecked upon the coast.
Wild thyme and savory set around their cell,
Sweet to the taste, and fragrant to the smell:
Set rows of rosemary with flowering stem,
And let the purple violets drink the stream.

Whether thou build the palace of thy bees
With twisted osiers, or with barks of trees,
Make but a narrow mouth; for, as the cold
Congeals into a lump the liquid gold,
So 'tis again dissolved by summer's heat;
And the sweet labors both extremes defeat.
And therefore, not in vain, the industrious kind
With dauby wax and flowers the chinks have lined,
And, with their stores of gathered glue, contrive
To stop the vents and crannies of their hive.
Not bird lime, or Idæan pitch, produce
A more tenacious mass of clammy juice.
    Nor bees are lodged in hives alone, but found
In chambers of their own beneath the ground:
Their vaulted roofs are hung in pumices,
And in the rotten trunks of hollow trees.
    But plaster thou the chinky hives with clay,
And leafy branches o'er their lodgings lay:
Nor place them where too deep a water flows,
Or where the yew, their poisonous neighbor, grows;
Nor roast red crabs, to offend the niceness of their nose;
Nor near the steaming stench of muddy ground;
Nor hollow rocks, that render back the sound,
And double images of voice rebound.
    For what remains, when golden suns appear,
And under earth have driven the winter year,
The wingèd nation wanders through the skies,
And o'er the plains and shady forest flies:

Then, stooping on the meads and leafy bowers,
They skim the floods, and sip the purple flowers.
Exalted hence, and drunk with secret joy,
Their young succession all their cares employ;
They breed, they brood, instruct, and educate,
And make provision for the future state:
They work their waxen lodgings in their hives,
And labor honey to sustain their lives.
    But when thou seest a swarming cloud arise,
That sweeps aloft, and darkens all the skies,
The motions of their hasty flight attend;
And know, to floods or woods, their airy march they bend.
Then melfoil beat, and honey-suckles pound;
With these alluring savors strew the ground;
And mix with tinkling brass the cymbal's droning sound.
Straight to their ancient cells, recalled from air,
The reconciled deserters will repair.
But, if intestine broils alarm the hive
(For two pretenders oft for empire strive),
The vulgar in divided factions jar;
And murmuring sounds proclaim the civil war.
Inflamed with ire, and trembling with disdain,
Scarce can their limbs their mighty souls contain.
With shouts, the coward's courage they excite,
And martial clangors call them out to fight:
With hoarse alarms the hollow camp rebounds,
That imitate the trumpet's angry sounds:
Then to their common standard they repair;

The nimble horsemen scour the fields of air;
In form of battle drawn, they issue forth,
And every knight is proud to prove his worth.
Prest for their country's honor and their king's,
On their sharp beaks they whet their pointed stings,
And exercise their arms, and tremble with their wings.
Full in the midst the haughty monarchs ride;
The trusty guards come up, and close the side;
With shouts the daring foe to battle is defied.
   Thus in the season of unclouded spring,
To war they follow their undaunted king;
Crowd through their gates; and, in the fields of light,
The shocking squadrons meet in mortal fight.
Headlong they fall from high, and wounded wound;
And heaps of slaughtered soldiers bite the ground.
Hard hail-stones lie not thicker on the plain,
Nor shaken oaks such showers of acorns rain.
With gorgeous wings, the marks of sovereign sway,
The two contending princes make their way;
Intrepid through the midst of danger go,
Their friends encourage, and amaze the foe.
With mighty souls in narrow bodies prest,
They challenge, and encounter breast to breast;
So fixed on fame, unknowing how to fly,
And obstinately bent to win or die,
That long the doubtful combat they maintain,
Till one prevails — for only one can reign.
Yet all these dreadful deeds, this deadly fray,

A cast of scattered dust will soon allay,
And undecided leave the fortune of the day.
  When both the chiefs are sundered from the fight,
Then to the lawful king restore his right;
And let the wasteful prodigal be slain,
That he, who best deserves, alone may reign.
With ease distinguished is the regal race:
One monarch wears an honest open face:
Shaped to his size, and godlike to behold,
His royal body shines with specks of gold,
And ruddy scales; for empire he designed,
Is better born, and of a nobler kind.
That other looks like nature in disgrace:
Gaunt are his sides, and sullen is his face;
And like their grisly prince appear his gloomy race,
Grim, ghastly, rugged, like a thirsty train
That long have traveled through a desert plain,
And spit from their dry chaps the gathered dust again.
The better brood, unlike the bastard crew,
Are marked with royal streaks of shining hue;
Glittering and ardent, though in body less:
From these, at 'pointed seasons, hope to press
Huge heavy honeycombs, of golden juice,
Not only sweet, but pure, and fit for use,
To allay the strength and hardness of the wine,
And with old Bacchus new metheglin join.
  But, when the swarms are eager of their play,
And loathe their empty hives, and idly stray,

Restrain the wanton fugitives, and take
A timely care to bring the truants back.
The task is easy — but to clip the wings
Of their high-flying arbitrary kings.
At their command, the people swarm away:
Confine the tyrant, and the slaves will stay.

Sweet gardens, full of saffron flowers, invite
The wandering gluttons, and retard their flight —
Besides the god obscene, who frights away,
With his lath sword, the thieves and birds of prey.
With his own hand, the guardian of the bees,
For slips of pines may search the mountain trees,
And with wild thyme and savory plant the plain,
Till his hard horny fingers ache with pain;
And deck with fruitful trees the fields around,
And with refreshing waters drench the ground.
   Now, did I not so near my labors end,
Strike sail, and hastening to the harbor tend,

My song to flowery gardens might extend —
To teach the vegetable arts, to sing
The Pæstan roses, and their double spring;
How succory drinks the running streams, and how
Green beds of parsley near the river grow;
How cucumbers along the surface creep,
With crooked bodies, and, with bellies deep —
The late narcissus, and the winding trail
Of bear's-foot, myrtles green, and ivy pale:
For, where with stately towers Tarentum stands,
And deep Galæsus soaks the yellow sands,
I chanced an old Corycian swain to know,
Lord of few acres, and those barren too,
Unfit for sheep or vines, and more unfit to sow;
Yet, laboring well his little spot of ground,
Some scattering pot-herbs here and there he found,
Which cultivated with his daily care,
And bruised with vervain, were his frugal fare.
Sometimes white lilies did their leaves afford,
With wholesome poppy-flowers, to mend his homely
   board;
For, late returning home, he supped at ease,
And wisely deemed the wealth of monarchs less:
The little of his own, because his own, did please.
   To quit his care, he gathered, first of all,
In spring the roses, apples in the fall;
And, when cold winter split the rocks in twain,
And ice the running rivers did restrain,

He stripped the bear's-foot of its leafy growth,
And, calling western winds, accused the spring of sloth.
He therefore first among the swains was found
To reap the product of his labored ground,
And squeeze the combs with golden liquor crowned.
His limes were first in flowers; his lofty pines,
With friendly shade, secured his tender vines.
For every bloom his trees in spring afford,
An autumn apple was by tale restored.
He knew to rank his elms in even rows,
For fruit the grafted pear-tree to dispose,
And tame to plums the sourness of the sloes.
With spreading planes he made a cool retreat,
To shade good fellows from the summer's heat.
But, straitened in my space, I must forsake
This task, for others afterwards to take.
    Describe we next the nature of the bees,
Bestowed by Jove for secret services,
When, by the tinkling sound of timbrels led
The king of heaven in Cretan caves they fed.
Of all the race of animals, alone
The bees have common cities of their own,
And common sons; beneath one law they live,
And with one common stock their traffic drive.
Each has a certain home, a several stall:
All is the state's; the state provides for all.
Mindful of coming cold, they share the pain,
And hoard, for winter's use, the summer's gain.

Some o'er the public magazines preside;
And some are sent new forage to provide:
These drudge in fields abroad; and those at home
Lay deep foundations for the labored comb,
With dew, narcissus leaves, and clammy gum.
To pitch the waxen flooring some contrive;
Some nurse the future nation of the hive:
Sweet honey some condense; some purge the grout;
The rest, in cells apart, the liquid nectar shut:
All, with united force, combine to drive
The lazy drones from the laborious hive:
With envy stung, they view each other's deeds:
With diligence the fragrant work proceeds.
    As when the Cyclops, at the almighty nod,
New thunder hasten for their angry god,
Subdued in fire the stubborn metal lies;
One brawny smith the puffing bellows plies,
And draws and blows reciprocating air:
Others to quench the hissing mass prepare:
With lifted arms they order every blow,
And chime their sounding hammers in a row;
With labored anvils Ætna groans below.
Strongly they strike; huge flakes of flames expire;
With tongs they turn the steel, and vex it in the fire.
If little things with great we may compare,
Such are the bees, and such their busy care:
Studious of honey each in his degree,
The youthful swain, the grave experienced bee —

That in the field; this, in affairs of state
Employed at home, abides within the gate,
To fortify the combs, to build the wall,
To prop the ruins, lest the fabric fall:
But, late at night, with weary pinions come
The laboring youth, and heavy laden, home.
Plains, meads, and orchards, all the day he plies;
The gleans of yellow thyme distend his thighs:
He spoils the saffron flowers; he sips the blues
Of violets, wilding blooms, and willow dews.

   Their toil is common, common is their sleep;
They shake their wings when morn begins to peep;
Rush through the city gates without delay;
Nor ends their work, but with declining day.
Then, having spent the last remains of light,
They give their bodies due repose at night,
When hollow murmurs of their evening bells
Dismiss the sleepy swains, and toll them to their cells.
When once in beds their weary limbs they steep,
No buzzing sounds disturb their golden sleep.
'Tis sacred silence all. Nor dare they stray,
When rain is promised, or a stormy day;
But near the city walls their watering take,
Nor forage far, but short excursions make.

   And as, when empty barks on billows float,
With sandy ballast sailors trim the boat;
So bees bear gravel-stones, whose poising weight
Steers through the whistling winds their steady flight.

But (what's more strange) their modest appetites,
Averse from Venus, fly the nuptial rites.
No lust enervates their heroic mind,
Nor wastes their strength on wanton womankind;
But in their mouths reside their genial powers:
They gather children from the leaves and flowers.
Thus make they kings to fill the regal seat,
And thus their little citizens create,
And waxen cities build, the palaces of state.
And oft on rocks their tender wings they tear,
And sink beneath the burdens which they bear:
Such rage of honey in their bosom beats;
And such a zeal they have for flowery sweets.

Thus though the race of life they quickly run,
Which in the space of seven short years is done,
The immortal line in sure succession reigns:
The fortune of the family remains;
And grandsires' grandsires the long list contains.
Besides, not Egypt, India, Media, more
With servile awe their idol king adore:
While he survives, in concord and content
The commons live, by no divisions rent;
But the great monarch's death dissolves the government.
All goes to ruin; they themselves contrive
To rob the honey, and subvert the hive.
The king presides, his subjects' toil surveys;
The servile rout their careful Cæsar praise:
Him they extol; they worship him alone;

They crowd his levees, and support his throne:
They raise him on their shoulders with a shout;
And, when their sovereign's quarrel calls them out,
His foes to mortal combat they defy,
And think it honor at his feet to die.
   Induced by such examples, some have taught
That bees have portions of ethereal thought —
Endued with particles of heavenly fires;
For God the whole created mass inspires.
Through heaven, and earth, and ocean's depth, he throws
His influence round, and kindles as he goes.
Hence flocks, and herds, and men, and beasts, and fowls,
With breath are quickened, and attract their souls,
Hence take the forms his prescience did ordain,
And into him at length resolve again.
No room is left for death: they mount the sky,
And to their own congenial planets fly.
   Now, when thou hast decreed to seize their stores,
And by prerogative to break their doors,
With sprinkled water first the city choke,
And then pursue the citizens with smoke.
Two honey harvests fall in every year:
First, when the pleasing Pleiades appear,
And, springing upward, spurn the briny seas:
Again, when their affrighted choir surveys
The watery Scorpion mend his pace behind,
With a black train of storms and winter wind,
They plunge into the deep, and safe protection find.

125

Prone to revenge, the bees, a wrathful race,
When once provoked, assault the aggressor's face,
And through the purple veins a passage find;
There fix their stings, and leave their souls behind.
  But, if a pinching winter thou foresee,
And would'st preserve thy famished family;
With fragrant thyme the city fumigate,
And break the waxen walls to save the state.
For lurking lizards often lodge, by stealth,
Within the suburbs, and purloin the wealth;
And worms, that shun the light, a dark retreat
Have found in combs, and undermined the seat;
Or lazy drones, without their share of pain,
In winter-quarters, free, devour the gain;
Or wasps infest the camps with loud alarms,
And mix in battle with unequal arms;
Or secret moths are there in silence fed;
Or spiders in the vault their snary webs have spread.
  The more oppressed by foes, or famine-pined,
The more increase thy care to save the sinking kind:
With greens and flowers recruit their empty hives,
And seek fresh forage to sustain their lives.
  But, since they share with man one common fate,
In health and sickness, and in turns of state —
Observe the symptoms. When they fall away,
And languish with insensible decay,
They change their hue; with haggard eyes they stare:
Lean are their looks, and shagged is their hair:

And crowds of dead, that never must return
To their loved hives, in decent pomp are borne:
Their friends attend the hearse; the next relations mourn.
The sick, for air, before the portal gasp,
Their feeble legs within each other clasp,
Or idle in their empty hives remain,
Benumbed with cold, and listless of their gain.
Soft whispers then, and broken sounds, are heard,
As when the woods by gentle winds are stirred;
Such stifled noise as the close furnace hides,
Or dying murmurs of departing tides.
This when thou seest, galbanean odors use,
And honey in the sickly hive infuse.
Through reeden pipes convey the golden flood,
To invite the people to their wonted food,
Mix it with thickened juice of sodden wines,
And raisins from the grapes of Psythian vines:
To these add pounded galls, and roses dry,
And, with Cecropian thyme, strong-scented centaury.
  A flower there is, that grows in meadow ground,
Amellus called, and easy to be found;
For, from one root, the rising stem bestows
A wood of leaves, and violet purple boughs:
The flower itself is glorious to behold,
And shines on altars like refulgent gold —
Sharp to the taste — by shepherds near the stream
Of Mella found; and thence they gave the name.
Boil this restoring root in generous wine,

And set beside the door, the sickly stock to dine.
But, if the laboring kind be wholly lost,
And not to be retrieved with care or cost;
'Tis time to touch the precepts of an art,
The Arcadian master did of old impart;
And how he stocked his empty hives again,
Renewed with putrid gore of oxen slain.
An ancient legend I prepare to sing,
And upward follow Fame's immortal spring:
   For, where with seven-fold horns mysterious Nile
Surrounds the skirts of Egypt's fruitful isle,
And where in pomp the sun-burnt people ride,
On painted barges, o'er the teeming tide,
Which, pouring down from Ethiopian lands,
Makes green the soil with slime, and black prolific sands:
That length of region, and large tract of ground,
In this one art a sure relief have found.
First, in a place by nature close, they build
A narrow flooring, guttered, walled, and tiled.
In this, four windows are contrived, that strike,
To the four winds opposed, their beams oblique.
A steer of two years old they take, whose head
Now first with burnished horns begins to spread:
They stop his nostrils, while he strives in vain
To breathe free air, and struggles with his pain.
Knocked down, he dies: his bowels, bruised within,
Betray no wound on his unbroken skin.
Extended thus, in this obscene abode

They leave the beast; but first sweet flowers are strewed
Beneath his body, broken boughs and thyme,
And pleasing cassia, just renewed in prime.
This must be done ere spring makes equal day,
When western winds on curling waters play;
Ere painted meads produce their flowery crops,
Or swallows twitter on the chimney tops.
The tainted blood, in this close prison pent,
Begins to boil, and through the bones ferment.
Then (wondrous to behold) new creatures rise,
A moving mass at first, and short of thighs);

Till, shooting out with legs, and imped with wings,
The grubs proceed to bees with pointed stings,
And, more and more affecting air, they try
Their tender pinions, and begin to fly:
At length, like summer storms from spreading clouds,
That burst at once, and pour impetuous floods —

Or flights of arrows from the Parthian bows,
When from afar they gall embattled foes —
With such a tempest through the skies they steer;
And such a form the wingèd squadrons bear.
    What god, O Muse! this useful science taught?
Or by what man's experience was it brought?
    Sad Aristæus from fair Tempè fled —
His bees with famine or diseases dead:
On Penëus' banks he stood, and near his holy head;
And, while his falling tears the stream supplied,
Thus, mourning, to his mother goddess cried:
"Mother Cyrene! mother, whose abode
Is in the depth of this immortal flood!
What boots it, that from Phœbus' loins I spring,
The third, by him and thee, from heaven's high king?
O! where is all thy boasted pity gone,
And promise of the skies to thy deluded son?
Why didst thou me, unhappy me, create,
Odious to gods, and born to bitter fate?
Whom scarce my sheep, and scarce my painful plough,
The needful aids of human life allow:
So wretched is thy son, so hard a mother thou!
Proceed, inhuman parent, in thy scorn;
Root up my trees; with blights destroy my corn;
My vineyards ruin, and my sheepfolds burn.
Let loose thy rage; let all thy spite be shown,
Since thus thy hate pursues the praises of thy son."
But, from her mossy bower below the ground,

His careful mother heard the plaintive sound —
Encompassed with her sea-green sisters round.
One common work they plied; their distaffs full
With carded locks of blue Milesian wool.
Spio, with Drymo brown, and Xantho fair,
And sweet Phyllodocè with long dishevelled hair;
Cydippè with Lycorias, once a maid,
And one that once had called Lucina's aid;
Clio and Beroë, from one father both;
Both girt with gold, and clad in particolored cloth;
Opis the meek, and Deïopeia proud
Nisæa lofty, with Ligea loud;
Thalia joyous, Ephyrè the sad,
And Arethusa, once Diana's maid,
But now (her quiver left) to love betrayed.
To these Clymenè the sweet theft declares
Of Mars; and Vulcan's unavailing cares;
And all the rapes of gods, and every love,
From ancient Chaos down to youthful Jove.

   Thus while she sings, the sisters turn the wheel,
Empty the woolly rock, and fill the reel.
A mournful sound again the mother hears;
Again the mournful sound invades the sisters' ears.
Starting at once from their green seats, they rise —
Fear in their heart, amazement in their eyes.
But Arethusa, leaping from her bed,
First lifts above the waves her beauteous head,
And, crying from afar, thus to Cyrene said:

131

"O sister, not with causeless fear possest!
No stranger voice disturbs thy tender breast.
'Tis Aristæus, 'tis thy darling son,
Who to his careless mother makes his moan.
Near his paternal stream he sadly stands,
With downcast eyes, wet cheeks, and folded hands,
Upbraiding heaven from whence his lineage came,
And cruel calls the gods, and cruel thee, by name."
   Cyrene, moved with love, and seized with fear,
Cries out, "Conduct my son, conduct him here:
'Tis lawful for the youth, derived from gods,
To view the secrets of our deep abodes."
At once she waved her hand on either side;
At once the ranks of swelling streams divide.
Two rising heaps of liquid crystal stand,
And leave a space betwixt of empty sand.
Thus safe received, the downward track he treads,
Which to his mother's watery palace leads.
With wondering eyes he views the secret store
Of lakes, that, pent in hollow caverns, roar:
He hears the crackling sounds of coral woods,
And sees the secret source of subterranean floods;
And where, distinguished in their several cells,
The fount of Phasis, and of Lycus, dwells;
Where swift Enipeus in his bed appears,
And Tiber his majestic forehead rears;
Whence Anio flows, and Hypanis profound
Breaks through the opposing rocks with raging sound;

Where Po first issues from his dark abodes,
And, awful in his cradle, rules the floods:
Two golden horns on his large front he wears,
And his grim face a bull's resemblance bears:
With rapid course he seeks the sacred main,
And fattens, as he runs, the fruitful plain.
　　Now, to the court arrived, the admiring son
Beholds the vaulted roofs of pory stone,
Now to his mother goddess tells his grief,
Which she with pity hears, and promises relief.
The officious nymphs attending in a ring,
With waters drawn from their perpetual spring,
From earthly dregs his body purify,
And rub his temples, with fine towels, dry;
Then load the tables with a liberal feast,
And honor with full bowls their friendly guest.
The sacred altars are involved in smoke;
And the bright choir their kindred gods invoke.
Two bowls the mother fills with Lydian wine;
Then thus: "Let these be poured with rites divine,
To the great authors of our watery line —
To father Ocean, this; and this (she said)
Be to the nymphs his sacred sisters paid,
Who rule the watery plains, and hold the woodland shade."
She sprinkled thrice, with wine, the Vestal fire,
Thrice to the vaulted roofs the flames aspire.
Raised with so blest an omen, she begun,
With words like these, to cheer her drooping son;

"In the Carpathian bottom, makes abode
The shepherd of the seas, a prophet, and a god.
High o'er the main in watery pomp he rides,
His azure car and finny coursers guides —
Proteus his name. — To his Pallenian port
I see from far the weary god resort.
Him, not alone, we river gods adore,
But aged Nereus hearkens to his lore.
With sure foresight, and with unerring doom,
He sees what is, and was, and is to come.
This Neptune gave him, when he gave to keep
His scaly flocks, that graze the watery deep.
Implore his aid; for Proteus only knows
The secret cause, and cure, of all thy woes.
But first the wily wizard must be caught:
For, unconstrained, he nothing tells for nought;
Nor is with prayers or bribes, or flattery bought.
Surprise him first, and with hard fetters bind;
Then all his frauds will vanish into wind.
I will myself conduct thee on thy way;
When next the southing sun inflames the day,
When the dry herbage thirsts for dews in vain,
And sheep, in shades, avoid the parching plain;
Then will I lead thee to his secret seat,
When, weary with his toil, and scorched with heat,
The wayward sire frequents his cool retreat.
His eyes with heavy slumber overcast —
With force invade his limbs, and bind him fast.

Thus surely bound, yet be not over bold;
The slippery god will try to loose his hold,
And various forms assume, to cheat thy sight,
And with vain images of beasts affright:
With foamy tusks will seem a bristly boar,
Or imitate the lion's angry roar:
Break out in crackling flames to shun thy snare,
Or hiss a dragon, or a tiger stare;
Or, with a wile thy caution to betray,
In fleeting streams attempt to slide away.
But, thou, the more he varies forms, beware
To strain his fetters with a stricter care,
Till, tiring all his arts, he turns again
To his true shape, in which he first was seen."
   This said, with nectar she her son anoints,
Infusing vigor through his mortal joints;
Down from his head the liquid odors ran:
He breathed of heaven, and looked above a man.
   Within a mountain's hollow womb there lies
A large recess, concealed from human eyes,
Where heaps of billows, driven by wind and tide,
In form of war, their watery ranks divide,
And there, like sentries set, without the mouth abide:
A station safe for ships, when tempests roar,
A silent harbor, and a covered shore.
Secure within resides the various god,
And draws a rock upon his dark abode.
Hither with silent steps, secure from sight,

The goddess guides her son, and turns him from the light:
Herself, involved in clouds, precipitates her flight.
  'Twas noon; the sultry Dog-star from the sky
Scorched Indian swains; the rivelled grass was dry;
The sun with flaming arrows pierced the flood,
And, darting to the bottom, baked the mud;
When weary Proteus, from the briny waves,
Retired for shelter to his wonted caves.
His finny flocks about their shepherd play,
And, rolling round him, spirt the bitter sea.
Unwieldily they wallow first in ooze,
Then in the shady covert seek repose.
Himself, their herdsman, on the middle mount,
Takes of his mustered flocks a just account.
So, seated on a rock, a shepherd's groom
Surveys his evening flocks returning home,
When lowing calves and bleating lambs from far,
Provoke the prowling wolf to nightly war.
  The occasion offers, and the youth complies:
For scarce the weary god had closed his eyes,
When, rushing on with shouts, he binds in chains
The drowsy prophet, and his limbs constrains.
He, not unmindful of his usual art,
First in dissembled fire attempts to part:
Then roaring beasts, and running streams, he tries,
And wearies all his miracles of lies:
But, having shifted every form to 'scape,
Convinced of conquest, he resumed his shape,

And, thus, at length, in human accent spoke:
"Audacious youth! what madness could provoke
A mortal man to invade a sleeping god?
What business brought thee to my dark abode?"
To this the audacious youth: "Thou knowest full well
My name and business, god; nor need I tell.
No man can Proteus cheat; but, Proteus, leave
Thy fraudful arts, and do not thou deceive.
Following the gods' command, I come to implore
Thy help, my perished people to restore."
The seer, who could not yet his wrath assuage,
Rolled his green eyes, that sparkled with his rage,
And gnashed his teeth, and cried, "No vulgar god
Pursues thy crimes, nor with a common rod.
Thy great misdeeds have met a due reward;
And Orpheus' dying prayers at length are heard.
For crimes not his, the lover lost his life,
And at thy hands requires his murdered wife:
Nor (if the Fates assist not) canst thou 'scape
The just revenge of that intended rape.
To shun thy lawless lust, the dying bride,
Unwary, took along the river's side,
Nor at her heels perceived the deadly snake,
That kept the bank, in covert of the brake.
But all her fellow-nymphs the mountains tear
With loud laments, and break the yielding air:
The realms of Mars remurmur all around,
And echoes to the Athenian shores rebound.

The unhappy husband, husband now no more,
Did on his tuneful harp his loss deplore,
And sought his mournful mind with music to restore.
On thee, dear wife, in deserts all alone,
He called, sighed, sung: his griefs with day begun,
Nor were they finished with the setting sun.
E'en to the dark dominions of the night
He took his way, through forests void of light,
And dared amidst the trembling ghosts to sing,
And stood before the inexorable king.
The infernal troops like passing shadows glide,
And, listening, crowd the sweet musician's side —
(Not flocks of birds, when driven by storms or night,
Stretch to the forest with so thick a flight) —
Men, matrons, children, and the unmarried maid,
The mighty hero's more majestic shade,
And youths, on funeral piles before their parents laid.
All these Cocytus bounds with squalid reeds,
With muddy ditches, and with deadly weeds;
And baleful Styx encompasses around,
With nine slow circling streams, the unhappy ground.
E'en from the depths of hell the damned advance;
The infernal mansions, nodding, seem to dance;
The gaping three-mouthed dog forgets to snarl.
The Furies hearken and their snakes uncurl
Ixion seems no more his pain to feel,
But leans attentive on his standing wheel.
All dangers past, at length the lovely bride

In safety goes, with her melodious guide,
Longing the common light again to share,
And draw the vital breath of upper air —
He first; and close behind him followed she;
For such was Proserpine's severe decree —
When strong desires the impatient youth invade,
By little caution and much love betrayed:
A fault, which easy pardon might receive,
Were lovers judges, or could hell forgive:
For near the confines of ethereal light,
And longing for the glimmering of a sight,
The unwary lover cast his eyes behind,
Forgetful of the law, nor master of his mind.
Straight all his hopes exhaled in empty smoke;
And his long toils were forfeit for a look.
Three flashes of blue lightning gave the sign
Of covenants broke; three peals of thunder join.
Then thus the bride: 'What fury seized on thee,
Unhappy man! to lose thyself and me?
Dragged back again by cruel Destinies,
An iron slumber shuts my swimming eyes.
And now farewell! Involved in shades of night,
For ever I am ravished from thy sight.
In vain I reach my feeble hands to join
In sweet embraces — ah! no longer thine!'
She said: and from his eyes the fleeting fair
Retired like subtle smoke dissolved in air,
And left her hopeless lover in despair.

In vain, with folding arms, the youth essayed
To stop her flight, and strain the flying shade:
He prays; he raves; all means in vain he tries,
With rage inflamed, astonished with surprise;
But she returned no more, to bless his longing eyes.
Nor would the infernal ferryman once more
Be bribed to waft him to the farther shore.
What should he do, who twice had lost his love?
What notes invent? what new petitions move?
Her soul already was consigned to fate,
And shivering in the leaky sculler sat.
For seven continued months, if fame say true,
The wretched swain his sorrows did renew:
By Strymon's freezing streams he sat alone:
The rocks were moved to pity with his moan:
Trees bent their heads to hear him sing his wrongs:
Fierce tigers couched around, and lolled their fawning
    tongues.
So, close in poplar shades, her children gone,
The mother nightingale laments alone,
Whose nest some prying churl had found, and thence
By stealth, conveyed the unfeathered innocence.
But she supplies the night with mournful strains;
And melancholy music fills the plains.
Sad Orpheus thus his tedious hours employs,
Averse from Venus, and from nuptial joys.
Alone he tempts the frozen floods, alone
The unhappy climes, where spring was never known:

142

He mourned his wretched wife, in vain restored,
And Pluto's unavailing boon deplored.
The Thracian matrons — who the youth accused
Of love disdained, and marriage-rites refused —
With furies and nocturnal orgies fired,
At length against his sacred life conspired.
Whom e'en the savage beasts had spared, they killed,
And strewed the mangled limbs about the field.
Then, when his head, from his fair shoulders torn,
Washed by the waters, was on Hebrus borne,
E'en then his trembling tongue invoked his bride
With his last voice, 'Eurydice,' he cried,
'Eurydice,' the rocks and river-banks replied."
   This answer Proteus gave; nor more he said,
But in the billows plunged his hoary head;
And, where he leaped, the waves in circles widely spread.
   The nymph returned, her drooping son to cheer,
And bade him banish his superfluous fear:
"For now (said she) the cause is known, from whence
Thy woe succeeded, and for what offence.
The nymphs, companions of the unhappy maid,
This punishment upon thy crimes have laid;
And sent a plague among thy thriving bees. —
With vows and suppliant prayers their powers appease:
The soft Napæan race will soon relent
Their anger, and remit the punishment.
The secret in an easy method lies;
Select four brawny bulls for sacrifice,

Which on Lycæus graze without a guide;
Add four fair heifers yet in yoke untried.
For these, four altars in their temple rear,
And then adore the woodland powers with prayer.
From the slain victims pour the streaming blood,
And leave their bodies in the shady wood:
Nine mornings thence, Lethæan poppy bring,
To appease the manes of the poet's king,
And, to propitiate his offended bride,
A fatted calf and a black ewe provide:
This finished, to the former woods repair."
His mother's precepts he performs with care;
The temple visits, and adores with prayer;
Four altars raises; from his herd he culls,
For slaughter, four the fairest of his bulls:
Four heifers from his female store he took,
All fair, and all unknowing of the yoke.
Nine mornings thence, with sacrifice and prayers,
The powers atoned, he to the grove repairs.
Behold a prodigy! for, from within
The broken bowels and the bloated skin,
A buzzing noise of bees his ears alarms;
Straight issue through the sides assembling swarms.
Dark as a cloud, they make a wheeling flight,
Then on a neighboring tree, descending, light:
Like a large cluster of black grapes they shew,
And make a large dependance from the bough.
   Thus have I sung of fields, of flocks, and trees,

And of the waxen work of laboring bees;
While mighty Cæsar, thundering from afar,
Seeks on Euphrates' banks the spoils of war;
With conquering arts asserts his country's cause,
With arts of peace the willing people draws;
On the glad earth the golden age renews,
And his great father's path to heaven pursues;
While I at Naples pass my peaceful days,
Affecting studies of less noisy praise,
And, bold through youth, beneath the beechen shade,
The lays of shepherds, & their loves, have played.

NOTES

These scattering observations are rather guesses at my author's meaning in some passages, than proofs that so he meant. The unlearned may have recourse to any poetical dictionary in English, for the names of persons, places, or fables, which the learned need not: but that little which I say is either new or necessary; and the first of these qualifications never fails to invite a reader, if not to please him.

JOHN DRYDEN

THE FIRST GEORGIC

PAGE 7   *Ye deities! who fields and plains protect*

After announcing the fourfold division of his poem, Virgil invokes a series of gods favorable to agriculture: sun and moon; Bacchus and Ceres; the Fauns and Dryads of the countryside; Neptune, who created the horse by striking the earth with his trident; Aristæus, a semi-divine hero who fostered cattle and fruit-trees; Pan, the shepherd god; Minerva (Pallas), inventress of the olive; Triptolemus, a culture hero sent by Ceres to teach men the use of the plough; Sylvanus, the spirit of woodlands, bearing an uprooted cypress; and all the deities of the land, especially Cæsar Augustus, divine emperor, destined to become the tutelary genius of Rome.

PAGE 10   *. . . when Deucalion hurled*
His mother's entrails on the desert world

Deucalion, the classical Noah, who with his wife Pyrrha were the sole survivors of the flood, created new men and women from stones ('his mother's entrails') flung over his shoulder; hence mankind is called a 'stony race'. See Dryden's translation of Ovid's *Metamorphoses*, Book I, 424-556.

PAGE 14   *Ere this no peasant vexed*

An allusion to the mythical Golden Age, when Saturn reigned as chief of the gods; with the coming of Jove, however, men were forced to toil for a livelihood and so learned arts and crafts.

PAGE 17   *The corn-devouring weasel*

The Latin reads: 'the weevil infests a huge heap of grain'. Dryden wrote 'Weezel', following a confusion of the words 'weevil' and 'weasel' which was common in the seventeenth century. Modernizing editors have done their bit to complete an instance of unnatural natural history.

PAGE 23   *And armed, against the skies, the sons of earth*

The Titans, 'Coeus, Iapetus, and savage Typhoeus', who tried by piling up mountains to scale the battlements of heaven and dethrone Jupiter.

PAGE 29   *The filmy gossamer now flits no more*

Meaning: Nor do light fleecy clouds pass across the sky.

PAGE 29   *Towering aloft, avenging Nisus flies*

Nisus, king of Megara, was betrayed by his daughter Scylla, who cut from his head the magic lock of red hair on which the safety of his throne depended. He was transformed into a sea-eagle and she into a smaller bird which the sea-eagle pursues. The meaning here is apparently that when the larger bird swoops the small bird dodges, and when the eagle mounts in order to swoop again, the small bird flies away in haste.

PAGE 33   *For this, the Emathian plains once more were strewed*

Virgil refers to the battles of Pharsalia and Philippi, both fought in the north of Greece. His geography, however, is less than exact, since one battle was fought in Macedonia (Emathia) and one in Thessaly. 'Rusty piles', five lines below, means javelins (*pila*).

PAGE 34   *And there Euphrates her soft offspring arms*

A reference to Mark Antony's campaign against the Parthians, and in the following line to Agrippa's expedition into Germany. Virgil is more alarmed, however, by the possibility of renewed civil war in Italy.

THE SECOND GEORGIC

PAGE 40   *Thus pears and quinces from the crab-tree come*

Dryden has reversed the situation. The Latin reads: 'often . . . we see . . . the transformed pear-tree bear engrafted apples, and stony cornel-berries reddening on the plum.'

PAGE 42   *The thin-leaved arbute, hazel-graffs receives*

Virgil's imagination seems to have run away with him at this point. Some of the combinations he lists are unknown to present-day nurserymen.

PAGE 44 *Nor our Italian vines produce the shape*

Discussion of the various types of grape leads naturally to comment on the quality of the vintage that comes from each. Virgil's 'wine-list' mentions at least two varieties not named elsewhere.

PAGE 45 *With Æthiops' hoary trees and woolly wood*

Virgil is speaking of cotton ('woolly wood') and, in the two lines that follow, of silk imported from the distant Orient. The Romans supposed that silk fibres were somehow combed from the leaves of trees ('fleecy forests').

PAGE 46 *No bulls, whose nostrils breathe a living flame*

The mythical hero Jason at Colchis yoked fire-breathing oxen to his plough and sowed dragon's teeth which produced a crop of armed warriors. Italy has enjoyed more peaceful beginnings.

PAGE 46 *There flows Clitumnus through the flowery plain*

The water of the Clitumnus was supposed to make cattle and sheep white and hence suitable for sacrifice.

PAGE 47 *Of the vast mound that binds the Lucrine lake*

This celebrated feat of engineering was accomplished by Agrippa. He made a harbor out of two small land-locked pools on the Campanian coast, facing the dike that separated Lucrinus from the sea with masonry and opening a channel for the admission of vessels.

PAGE 48 *And old Ascraean verse in Roman cities sing*

Meaning: And adapt the poetry of the Greek Hesiod to Roman conditions.

PAGE 60 *On whate'er side he turns his honest face*

The Latin *honestum caput* means literally 'comely head'.

PAGE 64 *Wine urged to lawless lust the Centaurs' train*

The whole history of the famous war between the Centaurs and the Lapithae may be found in Dryden's translation of 'The Twelfth Book of Ovid His Metamorphoses', 292–705.

PAGE 65 *From hence Astraea took her flight*

Dryden has substituted *Astraea* for the Latin *Iustitia*. The last traces of justice among men remain with the cultivators of the soil – an idea that strongly appealed to Thomas Jefferson.

THE THIRD GEORGIC

PAGE 75 *Thy fields, propitious Pales, I rehearse*

The Pales, god and goddess, were patrons of flocks and herds. Their festival occurred on April 21, which was also identified with the foundation-day of Rome. The 'Amphrysian shepherd' in the next line is Apollo Nomius. It was characteristic of Roman culture to link native Italian deities with the Greek gods.

PAGE 75 *All other themes*

The heroic legends of Hercules or Pelops, the love of Jupiter for Latona on the floating island of Delos – such themes as these, the common stock of poets, Virgil rejects. His intention is to apply the art of Greece to native Italian subjects. The poem he designs to write will be like a temple erected in honor of Cæsar.

PAGE 76 *The whorlbat*

An extravagance of mistranslation. Virgil was not speaking of Indian clubs or Irish shillelaghs, but of the *caestus*, a strip of rawhide loaded with iron or lead, which was used to arm the fists of boxers. A better vernacular rendering would be 'brass knuckles'.

PAGE 76   *Which interwoven Britons seem to raise*

Figures of captive Britons embroidered on the curtains of the imagined theatre.

PAGE 76   *The Nile shall flow beneath*

The Nile and Niphates, properly a mountain in Armenia, are geographical symbols of Octavian's victories in the Near East.

PAGE 80   *Such was the steed in Grecian poets famed*

A succession of famous horses: Cyllarus tamed by Pollux, one of the twin brothers of Helen of Troy; the two steeds of Mars (*Iliad*, xv, 119); the immortal team of Achilles (*Iliad*, xvi, 148); and finally the mythical story of Saturn, who took the form of a horse to prevent his wife Rhea from detecting his amour with Philyra.

PAGE 84   *This curse the jealous Juno did invent*

Jupiter turned Io, his love of the moment, into a heifer to escape Juno's observation, but Juno, not at all deceived, sent the gadfly to persecute Io. See Dryden's translation of Ovid's *Metamorphoses*, Book I, 769-1041.

PAGE 90   *What did the youth, when Love's unerring dart*

Leander, who swam the Hellespont to keep tryst with Hero, until drowned in a storm.

PAGE 94   *'Tis true, the fleece, when drunk with Tyrian juice*

Meaning: Woolen cloth dyed purple brings a high price.

PAGE 98   *The savage Scythian, and unwarlike Dutch*

Dryden, not Virgil, is responsible for this slur on the Dutch, whom he disliked.

153

THE FOURTH GEORGIC

PAGE 114   *And Procne, with her bosom stained in blood*

The swallow. Procne, married to King Tereus, killed their son Itys and served his flesh as a banquet for his father in retaliation for the rape of Philomela.

PAGE 114   *That, when the youthful prince, with proud alarm*

Virgil speaks of the queen bee as a 'king' and Dryden follows him. Until fairly recent times bees enjoyed a not wholly deserved reputation for chastity. Virgil alludes later to their gathering children from the leaves and flowers. An alternative theory was that they were spontaneously generated from the decaying carcasses of animals.

PAGE 117   *On their sharp beaks they whet their pointed stings*

No bee has ever succeeded in doing this. But bees do scrape their legs with their mandibles in a fashion that might mislead a casual observer.

PAGE 119   *For slips of pines may search the mountain trees*

Virgil's word here, and some forty lines later, is in all probability not *pinus*, but *tinus*. The laurustinus, a shrub something like laurel, is one that bees delight in.

PAGE 120   *I chanced an old Corycian swain to know*

This old man from Tarentum may have been one of the Cilician pirates domiciled in Calabria by Pompey. Cilicia enjoyed a great reputation for its gardens.

PAGE 121   *The king of heaven in Cretan caves they fed*

The infant Jupiter, hidden from Saturn in a cave on Mount Dicte, was fed with honey by the bees, while his crying was drowned out by the Curetes with their clashing timbrels.

PAGE 128   *The Arcadian master did of old impart*

Aristæus, legendary king of Arcadia, supposed to be the first to practice bee-keeping. The story that Virgil tells of him is unique.

PAGE 145   *Seeks on Euphrates' banks the spoils of war*

Shortly after the battle of Actium, Octavian made a triumphal excursion through Palestine and Syria.

PAGE 145   *The lays of shepherds, and their loves, have played*

Dryden's translation blurs the fact that the last line of the *Georgics* repeats, with the change of one word, the first line of the *Eclogues*: 'Of thee, Tityrus, under the spreading beech-tree's shade I sang.'